THE Aftermath OF THE French Revolution

JAMES R. ARNOLD

Clifton Park - Halfmoon Public Library
475 Moe Road
Clifton Park, New York 12065

TWENTY-FIRST CENTURY BOOKS   MINNEAPOLIS

Copyright © 2009 by James R. Arnold

3847

Twenty-First Century Books
A division of Lerner Publishing Group, Inc.
241 First Avenue North
Minneapolis, MN 55401 U.S.A.

Website address: www.lernerbooks.com

Library of Congress Cataloging-in-Publication Data

Arnold, James R.
    The aftermath of the French Revolution / by James R. Arnold.
        p.   cm. — (Aftermath of history)
    Includes bibliographical references and index.
    ISBN 978-0-8225-7598-6 (lib. bdg. : alk. paper)
        1. France—History—Revolution, 1789–1799—Influence—Juvenile literature.
    2. Europe—History—1789–1815—Juvenile literature. I. Title.
    DC148.A74 2009
    944.04—dc22   2007050828

Manufactured in the United States of America
1 2 3 4 5 6 – BP – 14 13 12 11 10 09

Contents

The King Must Die

H E WAS A DECENT MAN. He was not terribly smart, but he had the best interests of his family and his country at heart. The trouble was that he was the king of France, and for that reason alone, the new anti-monarchy revolutionary government, the National Convention, had condemned him to death. King Louis XVI knew that he was about to die. So, on the night of January 20, 1793, King Louis XVI said goodbye to his wife and queen, Marie Antoinette, and to his three young children.

On the cold, wet morning of January 21, a large force of cavalry (soldiers on horseback) escorted the king's green carriage to Paris's "Place de la Revolution (Revolution Square)." According to Henry Edgeworth, an English priest who traveled with the king, the carriage stopped in a large open space surrounded by cannons and by "an armed multitude [that] extended as far as the eye could reach."

As the king dismounted from his carriage, he saw soldiers guarding the guillotine (a machine with a heavy blade for beheading). He also saw an enormous crowd. Revolutionary leaders had wanted to conduct the execution of King Louis XVI as a public spectacle. They got their wish. The spectators saw three soldiers move to take off the king's brown coat and prepare him for the blade. The priest who accompanied Louis XVI recalled that the king "repulsed them with haughtiness—he undressed himself, untied his neckcloth, opened his shirt, and arranged it himself." At first, the king's composure startled the soldiers. Then they moved to tie his hands behind his back. The king resisted for a moment and then allowed the soldiers to proceed.

The priest reported that "The path leading to the scaffold was extremely rough and difficult to pass; the King was obliged to lean on my arm, and from the slowness with which he proceeded, I feared for

KING LOUIS XVI, IN WHITE VEST, BELOW, OF FRANCE WAS EXECUTED AT THE GUILLOTINE IN PARIS ON JANUARY 21, 1793, AS PORTRAYED IN THIS OIL PAINTING BY CHARLES BENAZECH (1767–1794).

a moment that his courage might fail; but what was my astonishment, when arrived at the last step, I felt that he suddenly let go my arm, and I saw him cross with a firm foot the breadth of the whole scaffold."

The eager, noisy crowd pressed forward to see better. Louis XVI stared at them and by his look alone silenced them. The king began to speak: "Frenchmen, I die innocent. It is from the scaffold and near God that I tell you so. I pardon my enemies; I desire that France. . . ."

The crowd never heard his final words. On orders from an officer, the drummers loudly beat their drums. The giant blade of the guillotine slid down the wooden frame and severed the king's head. A teenage assistant executioner held it aloft and paraded around the scaffold. People surged forward to dip pieces of clothing in the king's blood, a gruesome souvenir. Revolutionary leaders understood that they had taken a decisive step. There was no going back.

The revolutionary leaders knew that the execution of the French king presented a threat to all the hereditary monarchs of Europe. Some of those rulers were likely to wage war on France. But most revolutionary leaders did not care about the threat of war. They welcomed a war. One leader addressed the threat posed by foreign kings and issued a challenge: "We hurl at their feet, as a gage of battle, the head of a King."

The French Revolution was an event unlike any other. Back in 1776, American colonial rebels had started a revolution against their British rulers. They fought to cast off control by the distant govern-

FAST FACT

LIBERTÉ, ÉGALITÉ, FRATERNITÉ, OU LA MORT—"LIBERTY, EQUALITY, FRATERNITY, OR DEATH"— WAS THE SLOGAN OF THE FRENCH REVOLUTION. SHORTENED TO "LIBERTY, EQUALITY, FRATERNITY," IT IS THE OFFICIAL MOTTO OF THE MODERN FRENCH REPUBLIC.

ment of Great Britain. During that struggle, the American rebels received support from several European powers, including France. As a result of the American Revolution (1775–1783), the United States was formed as a new, independent nation. It created an enduring Constitution that separated powers among the executive, the legislative, and the judiciary branches of government. The American style of federal (elected) government employs a system of checks and balances to prevent any one branch of government from dominating the others.

French rebels began a revolution of their own in 1789. They fought against fellow French citizens to overthrow a social order based upon privilege. In contrast to the American rebels who had received vital assistance from Europe, French rebels fought against almost all of Europe. The French Revolution plunged the nation into a dark period of bloodshed. This was followed by the rise of a military dictator, Napoléon I, crowned as emperor in 1804.

The French Revolution changed the world. It was the first revolution of the modern world in which the ruling class had been overthrown. Before 1789 no one believed that an established social order could be overthrown. The French Revolution showed that it was possible.

CHAPTER 1

The Revolution Begins

IN 1789 FRANCE WAS THE most powerful nation in Europe. It had Europe's largest population, 26 million people, and a growing economy. A hereditary king, Louis XVI, ruled the nation. He was a good man who wanted to do the best for his people. France faced significant problems that would have challenged any leader. When the year began, neither the king nor anyone else could have guessed that a revolution was about to begin.

The French Revolution was not a single event. Rather, it was a series of developments over a period of years. Louis XVI became king in 1774. He inherited a financial crisis that became worse as time passed. France had fought three great wars over the previous eighty years. Most recently, in 1777 France had allied herself with American rebels to help the Americans win independence from Great Britain. In order to finance the wars, France had borrowed money. Massive borrowing continued after the American Revolution. By 1786 the pressing need to repay some of the loans produced a financial crisis.

At this time, a social and political system of privilege was well entrenched throughout France. The most powerful groups in society enjoyed the most privileges. For example, the Catholic clergy (church officials) had vast wealth but paid no direct taxes. The nobility (aristocrats, who inherit their titles and privileges) owned more than one-quarter of all land and taxed most of the rest of the land. They also resisted paying direct taxes. However, some members of these privileged groups had begun thinking in new ways because of the ideas that flowed from a new school of thought called the Enlightenment.

The Feudal System

THE FRENCH REVOLUTION WAS an attack against privilege. That privilege came from the time the feudal system prevailed in western Europe, from the eighth century to the fifteenth century. Under feudalism lords owned all land, which they distributed to vassals—men who performed specific military or other services. The ultimate lord was the king. Lords and vassals were bound to one another by personal loyalty.

A piece of land given to a vassal was called a fief. The vassal did not own the land but had to provide regular goods or services to the landlord. Vassals could leave their fiefdoms to their heirs, but the land reverted to the lord if a vassal died without heirs. Lords also gave land to churches or monasteries, whose occupants were then required to pray for the landlords.

Serfs, or peasants bound to the land, lived on and farmed the land. Landlords exercised total power over the serfs, who were not free to leave the land. Serfs also had to give a share of their produce to the landlord. Lords and their vassals formed semi-independent governments within the borders of their nation. Feudalism also existed outside of western Europe, in such places as Japan, eastern Europe, and Russia.

The philosophers and writers of the Enlightenment emphasized reason and justice over religious faith and questioned traditional values. The Enlightenment influenced both the growing French middle class and some members of the nobility and clergy. The middle class, known as the bourgeoisie (a French word meaning "town dwellers" that later entered the English language), wanted more of a say in the government. At the same time, some of the nobility actually began to question whether they deserved their own privileged position.

In November 1788, the French statesman Emmanuel-Joseph Sieyès published "Essay on Privileges." It began with the rousing words, "It has been said that privileges mean exemption for those who hold them and discouragement for everyone else." Sieyès proceeded to examine the nature of society and the common interests

> *"Were the government more enlightened, it would see that a society needs . . . nothing more than citizens living and acting beneath the shelter of the law."*
>
> —Emmanuel-Joseph Sieyès, 1788

that caused people to form laws and governments. He argued that granting privileges degraded the majority of citizens. Sieyès presented a radical challenge to the noble class and their privileges: "Were the government more enlightened, it would see that a society needs . . . nothing more than citizens living and acting beneath the shelter of the law." In short, he argued, there was no need for the nobility.

IN HIS "ESSAY ON PRIVILEGES" (1788), FRENCH STATESMAN
EMMANUEL SIEYÈS PRESENTED A RADICAL CHALLENGE TO THE
FRENCH NOBLE CLASS. THIS FRENCH ILLUSTRATION DATES TO THE
NINETEENTH CENTURY.

THE KING SUMMONS THE ESTATES GENERAL

In the 1700s, France was an absolute monarchy. King Louis XVI did not share his power with anybody. Consequently, he believed that only he had the right to impose taxes to raise money to repay France's debts. However, Louis XVI also knew that he had to listen to his advisers when making important decisions. He and his ministers had come to realize that the only way they could govern effectively was with the cooperation of the nation's elite classes. However, this elite, or aristocracy, feuded with the king over the issue of raising additional taxes. Eventually, the aristocracy gained enough power to insist that the king summon the Estates General. As France's three-part representative body, the Estates General was composed of the Catholic clergy, the nobility, and the rest of the country's population. The aristocracy intended to use the meeting of the Estates General to reduce the king's power.

> **FAST FACT**
>
> THE FIRST ESTATE REPRESENTED 130,000 MEMBERS OF THE CATHOLIC CLERGY. THE SECOND ESTATE REPRESENTED 400,000 MEMBERS OF THE NOBILITY. THE THIRD ESTATE REPRESENTED MOST EVERYONE ELSE IN FRANCE.

According to French tradition, the king was supposed to consider the opinions expressed by the Estates General when making decisions, but the Estates General had not met since 1614. In each chamber of France's Estates General, delegates met to reach a consensus. Delegates for the First Estate represented 130,000 members of the Catholic clergy. Delegates for the Second Estate represented 400,000 members of the nobility. Delegates for the Third Estate represented everyone else. In other words, the Third Estate represented most of the people of France.

The Third Estate included people of different classes. At the top were wealthy people such as bankers, financiers, business owners, and industrialists. They often led lives that resembled those of the wealthiest members of the nobility. But since they had not been born into nobility, they were not allowed to pursue careers in the army or jobs in the top levels of government.

The Third Estate also included much less wealthy bourgeois people. Some were skilled craftsmen. Others were doctors, lawyers, artists, and writers. Regardless of their class, members of the Third Estate held the least status within the Estates General. The Third Estate was a permanent political minority since the other two estates acted together, thereby outvoting the Third Estate two to one.

Many among the bourgeoisie belonged to clubs that discussed and debated important new ideas. These clubs became centers of revolutionary spirit. The clubs helped spread a demand for more rights for the Third Estate. The Third Estate began to see itself as representative of the entire nation. It demanded complete equality before the law. Sieyès, who had previously gained public attention with his "Essay on Privileges," was a member of the Third Estate.

In January 1789, Sieyès wrote "What Is the Third Estate?" the most influential pamphlet of the prerevolutionary period. In it he asked and answered three vital questions: "1. What is the Third Estate? Everything. 2. What has it been up to now in the political order? Nothing. 3. What does it ask? To become something." To become "something," the Third Estate asked to have as many representatives in the Estates General as the other two estates combined.

The First Estate, the clergy, did not want to yield its top position. The Second Estate, the nobility, was possibly willing to accept equal taxation. But it refused to give up its other privileges. King Louis XVI might have been able to avoid national disaster if he had worked to make sweeping reforms. Instead, he made only small concessions and backed those who held privileged positions, namely the members of the First and Second Estates.

With the king's refusal to support the Third Estate, the Third Estate took action on June 17, 1789. It declared itself the National Assembly and invited the other two estates to join. They refused. King Louis XVI prevented the delegates to the Third Estate from gathering in their meeting chamber. So, the Third Estate assembled on a nearby indoor tennis court. Here, on June 20, 1789, they pledged an oath never to disband until France had a new constitution. In other words, the Third Estate proclaimed itself France's new constitution maker. It had seized a power formerly held by the king. This was revolution.

The king responded three days later. He made some concessions, but most important, he repeated that the privileges of the nobility

ON JUNE 20, 1789, MEMBERS OF THE THIRD ESTATE, AS PICTURED IN THIS NINETEENTH-CENTURY OIL PAINTING BY AUGUSTE CLOUDER, PLEDGED NOT TO DISBAND UNTIL FRANCE HAD A NEW CONSTITUTION.

would not change. One of the delegates of the Third Estate told the king's representative that "it would take bayonets" to make the Third Estate accept the king's position. Indeed, the king foresaw the potential for violence and began to assemble troops around Paris to deal with what he viewed as an arrogant Third Estate.

STORMING OF THE BASTILLE

About 16 percent of all French citizens lived in cities at this time. Paris, with a population of between 600,000 and 650,000, was by far the largest and most influential city. The city had a long tradition of popular protest. When Parisians learned of the conflict between the Third Estate and King Louis XVI, they formed a militia (a volunteer citizen army), soon to be called the National Guard.

FAST FACT

NINETY-EIGHT CIVILIANS DIED IN THE STORMING OF THE BASTILLE ON JULY 14, 1789.

When they learned that the king was assembling soldiers, they took action by marching on a fortress in Paris called the Bastille.

The Bastille was a powerful symbol. The king had the power to send prisoners to the Bastille, where they were held in secret and without trial. Thus, it was a symbol of the king's arbitrary rule (not governed by principle or law). A mob arrived at the Bastille on July 14, 1789, and demanded weapons from the soldiers there. The fortress commander, a nobleman named Bernard de Launay, ordered his soldiers to resist. Ninety-eight civilians died in the fight, but the mob pressed ahead and overran the Bastille. They hauled Launay outside and decapitated him. Later, the mob tore apart the Bastille stone by stone. (Modern France continues to celebrate this event by marking July 14 as Bastille Day.)

ON JULY 14, 1789, A PARIS MOB STORMED AND DESTROYED THE BASTILLE PRISON, AS SHOWN IN THIS EIGHTEENTH-CENTURY FRENCH SCHOOL OIL PAINTING.

When a court official told the king about the fall of the Bastille, he remarked with astonishment: "Good God! That is a revolt!" The official replied, "No Sire, it is a revolution." At the time, the capture of the Bastille revealed the king's weakness. With rebels in control of Paris, it marked the beginning of the collapse of the king's rule. The king's brother and many of his most important advisers fled the country.

THE AFTERMATH OF THE FRENCH REVOLUTION

THE AUGUST DECREES

The National Constituent Assembly (the National Assembly had re-named itself on July 9, 1789) worked to create a new society. In one session on August 4, 1789, the assembly abolished the feudal system and rescinded the privileges held by the clergy and the nobility. Yet the assembly was not ready to overthrow the king. Still, in a matter of hours, the assembly had eliminated the basis of the old social order. In the words of one historian, "much of the fabric of French social life had been condemned to destruction in the most radical few hours of the entire Revolution."

Later in August 1789, the assembly passed the Declaration of the Rights of Man and Citizen. Its principles mostly came from the Constitution of the United States. In seventeen short articles, the French declaration pronounced that all people were free and equal, subject to law, free to own property, free to express opinions, and entitled to participate in the political process.

FAST FACT

IN THE AFTERMATH OF THE STORMING OF THE BASTILLE ON JULY 14, 1789, PARISIANS FORMED A NATIONAL GUARD OF PARIS. SOON OTHER CITIES FOLLOWED AND THE FRENCH NATIONAL GUARD WAS BORN. THE NATIONAL GUARD WAS AT FIRST COMPOSED ONLY OF VOLUNTEERS. LATER, MEN WERE DRAFTED INTO THE NATIONAL GUARD.

The declaration made no provision for equality between men and women. Women played important public roles during 1789, but the men of the French Revolution generally believed that women belonged in the roles of wife and mother. Politics was for men only.

Meanwhile, rumors spread that the aristocracy was conspiring against the common people. These rumors caused unrest among the peasant class, which lived in the cities and in the countryside. The peasants paid taxes for which they gained little benefit. They hated the feudal lords who stood directly over them. Yet most did not blame the king for society's troubles.

However, a terrible harvest the year before had caused the price of bread, the staple food, to rise steeply. Workers typically ate three pounds of bread each day. They spent up to half their wages just on bread, but the lines to purchase bread had been growing longer and longer. This lack of bread in turn caused a famine. The peasant class was ready for change.

The desire for change came at a time when law and order were breaking down throughout France. An American diplomat in Paris, Gouverneur Morris, had played an important role in the American Revolution. What he saw taking place in the streets of Paris shocked him. While taking an after-dinner walk, he encountered a mob triumphantly parading about with a slaughtered seventy-year-old man, "the head on a pike, the body dragged naked on the earth." The victim's "crime" had been to accept a place in the king's government. The mob dragged the mutilated remains to the home of the man's son-in-law. He was also killed and cut to pieces, the populace carrying about the mangled fragments with savage joy. On seeing this, Morris exclaimed, "Gracious God! what a people!"

The display of a severed head on a pike was in part due to the wild emotions of the mob. But it also had a political purpose: to show other revolutionaries that they had power to make change; to

FAST FACT

GOUVERNEUR MORRIS WAS THE U.S. MINISTER PLENIPOTENTIARY TO FRANCE FROM 1792 TO 1794. HIS DIARIES WRITTEN DURING THAT TIME PROVIDE HISTORIANS WITH A UNIQUE CHRONICLE OF THE FRENCH REVOLUTION.

GOUVERNEUR MORRIS WAS AN AMERICAN DIPLOMAT IN PARIS IN THE 1700S. THIS PASTEL ON PAPER PAINTING WAS DONE BY JAMES SHARPLES IN 1810.

energize neutral spectators to act in revolutionary ways; and to terrorize foes of the revolution.

"TO VERSAILLES!"

Meanwhile, outside of Paris, King Louis XVI ordered a regiment of infantry (foot soldiers) to come to his palace at Versailles to protect him.

All French forces were supposed to wear ornaments called cockades on their hats. These cockades were blue, red, and white (the colors of the modern French flag). Blue and red were the colors of Paris. White was the color of the king. At a banquet before the royal family, the loyal regiment tore off their tricolor cockades and stomped on them. They replaced them with a simple white cockade.

> ## FAST FACT
>
> CONSTRUCTION OF THE PALACE OF VERSAILLES BEGAN IN 1661. THE PALACE WAS BUILT FOR LOUIS XIV ON THE SITE OF A HUNTING LODGE. VERSAILLES BECAME THE PRINCIPAL RESIDENCE OF THE FRENCH KINGS FROM 1678 TO 1793.

Morris, the American diplomat, wrote that the news of the behavior of the king's loyal regiment "spread like fire among the famishing crowds." He reported his sense of what people on the street were saying: "Aristocrats had trampled their colors under foot. They had bread and to spare; they feast while we starve. Let us go to Versailles and demand bread."

An army officer, Paul Thiébault, confirmed Morris's description. Thiébault described how Paris was "a volcanic soil from which torrents of flame were ready to burst out at the least shock. . . . In the midst of a general tumult some cries were distinctly heard: the first was 'Bread!' the second 'Arms!' the third 'To Versailles!' the fourth 'The King to Paris!'"

On October 6, 1789, thousands of women led a mob on a march to the king's palace at Versailles. Like the Bastille, Versailles was a powerful symbol. It represented both the king's arbitrary rule and, more important, a social system dominated by the privileged nobility. For these reasons, it was easy to convince the mob to march on Versailles. There, the mob stormed the hall of the National

Assembly to demand bread. An eyewitness recalled that soon the hall was "full of women and men armed with scythes, sticks, and pikes." The king agreed to meet with the mob's leaders. He satisfied their demands with promises of bread, and it seemed that peace would prevail. Instead, at dawn the next day, the mob invaded the king's royal quarters and threatened the life of the queen.

King Louis XVI's marriage to the Austrian princess Marie Antoinette had never been popular in France. It did not help her popularity that she led a showy, extravagant life. The mob hunted for the queen, promising to kill her if they found her. Royal guards and armed thugs exchanged blows, and a handful of people were killed. Fortunately for the royal family, a force of national guardsmen commanded by the Marquis de Lafayette prevented a larger massacre. Lafayette's guardsmen, surrounded by the mob, escorted the king back to Paris. All along the road to Paris, people hailed the king with the title "the Baker." This was a hopeful title alluding "to the plenty which was to reign in Paris" when the king arrived. He would make sure that there would be bread to bake. More ominously, the mob

"Let Them Eat Cake"

MARIE ANTOINETTE HAS GONE down in history as the maker of this callous and insensitive remark, allegedly in response to the complaint that the French people had no bread to eat. The same remark had been attributed to the wife of a previous king, Louis XIV. More likely, revolutionaries fabricated the remark and falsely attributed it to Marie Antoinette in order to incite people against the monarchy. Marie Antoinette was already widely hated for spending lavishly and for being Austrian. Austria was a historic enemy of France.

used the severed heads of the king's bodyguards as standards, "and these ghastly trophies were hailed with hideous chants," a French officer later recalled. When he arrived in Paris, Louis XVI occupied an old palace called the Tuileries. For all practical purposes, he was now a prisoner of the Parisian mob.

CHAPTER 2

Sweeping Changes Come to France

DURING 1790, IN ITS FIRST year of operation, the Constituent Assembly made sweeping changes. The assembly redrew the map of France, replacing ancient political boundaries that created thirty-four provinces with eighty-three new departments. From this point forward, all officials including councillors, administrators, legal officers, and judges of the local courts were to be elected by the people instead of appointed by the king. In this way, municipalities all the way down to the smallest village would gain local autonomy, or self-rule.

The Constituent Assembly also began a major restructuring and reorganizing of the Catholic Church in France. This effort began with the July 1790 adoption of "The Civil Constitution of the Clergy." Under this measure, the government took possession of church property. This was no small step, as the Catholic Church at the time owned about 10 percent of all land in France. The assembly also took

THE CONSTITUENT ASSEMBLY BEGAN A MAJOR RESTRUCTURING OF
THE CATHOLIC CHURCH IN FRANCE IN THE 1790s. THIS ANONYMOUS
COLORED ENGRAVING IS FROM THE 1700s.

away the church's independence. From this point forward, bishops
and priests were to be paid employees of the state rather than of
the church. As part of this change, they would have to swear loyalty
to the state. This was one of the most controversial parts of the
new measure. Many clergy understood that their first loyalty to God
might come in conflict with a sworn oath to the state. In addition,
the church lost its hold on the appointment of priests and bishops.
That task had always fallen to the pope, who was the church's spiritual leader. Instead, people outside the Catholic Church—including

> "I belong to my flock in life and in death."
>
> —an anonymous French clergyman, 1790

Protestants, Jews, and atheists—would have a say in naming Catholic clergy. The clergy loudly objected to these stunning changes.

In November 1790, the Constituent Assembly imposed a loyalty oath. Half of France's priests, almost all the bishops, and many of the nuns refused to take the oath. A typical clergyman said, "I can no more renounce the spiritual contract which binds me to my Church than I can renounce the promise of my baptism. . . . I belong to my flock in life and in death." The pope publicly denounced the Civil Constitution of the Clergy. Many devout, rural Catholics also opposed the changes.

The Civil Constitution of the Clergy created an important political battleground. In the words of historian William Doyle, "For the first time the revolutionaries forced fellow citizens to choose; to declare themselves publicly for or against the new order." Prorevolutionary "patriots" worked hard to enforce the new laws through political clubs. On the other side, counterrevolutionaries, or opponents, linked their efforts with those who wanted to defend the traditional powers and rights of the Catholic Church. For example, members of the nobility, or royalists, who wanted to return to power found support from devout Catholics.

FAST FACT

AROUND 1790, THE CATHOLIC CHURCH OWNED ABOUT 10 PERCENT OF ALL LAND IN FRANCE.

THE KING'S FLIGHT

During this time of unrest and violence, increasing numbers of the French nobility fled the country. Many joined the ranks of émigré (exiled) forces. These forces hoped to free and restore the king of France as well as to reestablish their own privileged place in society.

The Jacobin Club

MEMBERS OF THE NATIONAL ASSEMBLY in 1789 formed the Jacobin Club, named after the Paris building in which it first met. Within a year, the club had given rise to a nationwide network of Societies of the Friends of the Constitution, also called Jacobin clubs. The Jacobins dominated national politics during the French Revolution, becoming more radical as time went on. They presided over the arrest and execution of anyone deemed to be an enemy of the republic. These events, which took place between 1793 and 1794, became known as the Terror. When the violence ended in July 1794, the Jacobins quickly lost influence to more moderate factions (groups).

THE NATIONAL ASSEMBLY FORMED THE SOCIETIES OF THE FRIENDS OF THE CONSTITUTION, OR THE JACOBIN CLUBS. THESE GROUPS DOMINATED FRENCH NATIONAL POLITICS DURING THE REVOLUTION. THIS NINETEENTH-CENTURY ENGRAVING IS BY LOUIS BLANC.

From the safety of foreign territory along France's eastern border, they made their plans.

The émigrés' attempt to free the king from captivity in Paris came on June 20, 1791. It was poorly organized. The king and his family fled eastward and almost reached the safety of foreign territory. Their flight ended at Varennes in eastern France, where they were captured and led back to Paris as prisoners.

The Constituent Assembly debated what to do. Up until this point, most delegates had thought in terms of forming a new government with a king as head of state. Yet they were deeply suspicious of Louis XVI and his remaining advisers. The more radical delegates, called the Jacobins and the Cordeliers, wanted to put the king on trial. The more moderate delegates, called the Feuillants, worried about how the public would respond once it learned that the king had tried to flee the country. They feared an angry response and the possibility of violence. The moderates won the day. An official committee claimed that the king was innocent of wrongdoing and had been abducted against his will. This finding, for the moment, saved the monarchy.

The king's acquittal angered the Paris mob. The Jacobins and the Cordeliers organized a mass demonstration in Paris. On July 17, 1791, a huge crowd gathered to demand the removal of the king. Egged on by fiery political speeches, the crowd became unruly. The National Guard fired into the crowd, killing about thirty to fifty people. The event prompted the moderates in the Constituent Assembly to turn against the radicals. Already, the split within the Constituent Assembly over the future form of French government and society was becoming obvious.

In September 1791, the Constituent Assembly passed a new constitution. The constitution placed sovereign power, the power to rule a nation, in the hands of the people rather than in the hands of the king. Louis XVI thus became a servant of France, and the new constitution subjected him and all other officials to the rule of law. King Louis XVI had no choice but to accept the new constitution even though, by its terms, he lost most of his power.

A new Legislative Assembly took over from the Constituent Assembly. While nobles and clerics (members of the clergy) had made up half of the Constituent Assembly, only a handful remained in the Legislative Assembly. The deputies in the Legislative Assembly were solidly middle and upper class. Most owned property. Many were lawyers. They had experience in local politics. Many belonged to the Jacobin clubs or to the National Guard or had served in local judiciary and administrative posts. At the local level, they had learned who the enemies of the Revolution were: the priests and the émigrés.

The Émigrés

MEMBERS OF THE UPPER class fled France during the Revolution and became political refugees in the German states or in England. They feared, with good reason, that if they stayed in France, they would be killed. Most desired to see a return of the old regime under which they had prospered. After the 1793 execution of King Louis XVI, some émigrés formed military units to fight against France.

MEMBERS OF THE FRENCH UPPER CLASS FLED FRANCE DURING THE REVOLUTION AND BECAME ÉMIGRÉS (POLITICAL REFUGEES) IN THE GERMAN STATES AND IN ENGLAND.

So, on November 9, 1791, the Legislative Assembly issued a decree against the émigrés. By its terms, all French citizens living abroad were suspected of plotting against the nation. If they did not return, they were to be deemed guilty of a capital crime (a crime punishable by death). However, the king still possessed the power to veto legislation. Three days later, Louis XVI vetoed this decree. On November 29, 1791, the Legislative Assembly issued a decree against priests. Twenty days later, the king vetoed it. A situation where the assembly and the king adamantly disagreed could not endure.

CHAPTER 3

War with Europe

THE GROWING STRENGTH of the revolutionary movement inside France surprised Europe's monarchs. For hundreds
of years, France had been a powerful rival. Britain and France had
been bitter foes for centuries. Throughout the 1600s and even into
the 1700s, some of the nations on the European continent had also
fought France.

All of those conflicts followed conventional patterns. They were
limited wars, fought for defined objectives such as the possession of
a small amount of territory. The revolution inside France appeared to
upset all of these historical patterns. It presented Europe with a new
challenge. Europe's monarchs wondered if the changes taking place
in France could happen in their own countries. The solution seemed
to be to force France to return to the old patterns.

Accordingly, on August 27, 1791, King Frederick William II of
Prussia (in what is modern Germany) and Emperor Joseph Leopold

II of Austria issued a declaration. The Declaration of Pillnitz let the world know that Prussia and Austria were ready to join with other European nations to restore Louis XVI to power in France. If, during this effort, they managed to acquire some French territory for themselves, that was a useful bonus. But grabbing more territory was a secondary objective. First and foremost, Austria and Prussia wanted to take advantage of the military and political chaos to invade France and restore the king. In addition, French émigrés urged

THIS NINETEENTH-CENTURY ENGRAVING FROM PRUSSIA DEPICTS KING FREDERICK WILLIAM II OF PRUSSIA, LEFT, AND EMPEROR JOSEPH LEOPOLD II OF AUSTRIA, CENTER, MEETING WITH HOLY ROMAN EMPEROR FRIEDRICH AUGUSTUS III TO ISSUE THE DECLARATION OF PILLNITZ. THEY HOPED TO RESTORE LOUIS XVI TO THE THRONE OF FRANCE.

action to restore the monarchy. They also said that an invading army would find support from many French people who shared the desire to restore the king.

At this stage, King Louis XVI still had the constitutional power to conduct foreign policy. France's Legislative Assembly urged him to act against the émigrés who were gathering just outside of French territory along the Rhine River to the east. The king understood it would be politically unwise to challenge the legislature, so he dutifully responded by threatening the leaders of Mainz and Trier, two Prussian towns just across the Rhine. Austria, in turn, announced that it would march against France if the French acted against Mainz and Trier.

Jacques-Pierre Brissot, a Parisian journalist, was a leading deputy in the Legislative Assembly. His allies came from Bordeaux in southwestern France and were called the Brissotins. (They were later known as the Girondins, after a river that runs through Bordeaux.) These Bordeaux deputies were wealthy merchants. They believed that war would be good for the economy and would put money in their pockets. So, they supported Brissot when he argued repeatedly that war was necessary to consolidate the Revolution.

FAST FACT

AUSTRIA AND PRUSSIA FORMED AN ALLIANCE AGAINST FRANCE ON FEBRUARY 7, 1792.

Austria's threat, coming on top of the Declaration of Pillnitz, provided ammunition for Brissot. It allowed him to claim that foreign leaders obviously wanted to crush the Revolution. Brissot and his supporters responded to the Austrian threat with their own ultimatum. They told

THE AFTERMATH OF THE FRENCH REVOLUTION

JACQUES-PIERRE BRISSOT, A PARISIAN JOURNALIST, BELIEVED
FOREIGN WARS WERE NECESSARY TO CONSOLIDATE THE REVOLUTION.
THIS PORTAIT OF HIM, BY AN ANONYMOUS PAINTER, IS FROM THE
EARLY NINETEENTH CENTURY.

Louis XVI to tell Austria that, unless Austria renounced its threats,
there would be war.

On February 7, 1792, Austria and Prussia made an alliance
against France. Then, Austrian and Prussian soldiers began marching toward the French frontier.

The Revolutionary Wars

In response, the Legislative Assembly of France declared war against Austria on April 20, 1792. The subsequent series of wars became known in history as the Revolutionary Wars, or the wars of the French Revolution. The Legislative Assembly described the war as defensive—pitting a free people against an aggressive foe. The Legislative Assembly pledged that French forces would never be used against the liberty of any people. It also pledged that French forces would avoid harming innocent people and their property. During the Revolutionary Wars, France would break both of these pledges.

The decision to engage in war had huge consequences for all of the participants. King Louis XVI mistakenly believed that as soon as foreign enemies threatened France, the French people would rally to him. Austrian and Prussian leaders believed that when their armies invaded France, many French people would rally to support them. France's revolutionary government, led by Brissot and his supporters, believed that the threat of foreign invasion would drive the French people to support the Revolution.

The decision for war was wildly popular among the deputies of the Legislative Assembly. They saw war as the chance to teach all of Europe to avoid interfering with the Revolution. It was also an opportunity to crush the émigrés. Finally, it was a way to deal with internal enemies, because war forced people to decide where they stood. It was no longer possible to claim loyalty to France while opposing the Revolution.

Those who had created the Revolution said that those who criticized it were traitors. This stance put King Louis XVI in a bind. Whenever he refused to accept new rulings from the Legislative Assembly, people wondered if he himself was a traitor.

KING LOUIS XVI MISTAKENLY BELIEVED THAT THE FRENCH PEOPLE
WOULD RALLY TO HIM AS SOON AS FOREIGN POWERS THREATENED FRANCE.
THIS PORTRAIT OF KING LOUIS XVI WAS DONE BY DUPLESSIS-JOSEPH
SIFFRED IN THE LATE EIGHTEENTH CENTURY.

"La Marseillaise"

"LA MARSEILLAISE," THE NATIONAL anthem of modern France, began as a war song. A French army officer, Claude-Joseph Rouget de Lisle, composed it in 1792 after France declared war on Austria. He called it the "Battle Song of the Army of the Rhine." When soldiers from the French seaport of Marseilles sang it as they marched into Paris, the Song quickly spread throughout France as an anthem of the Revolution. (*La Marseillaise* is French for "The Song of Marseilles.") It was later banned, but in 1879, France adopted "La Marseillaise" as its national anthem. It was again banned in France under the German occupation of World War II (1939–1945), before being reinstated as the nation's official anthem.

"La Marseillaise" became a rallying cry to resistance movements and revolutions around the world. For example, condemned labor activists in Chicago, Illinois, sang the song on their way to their execution in 1887. After the Russian Revolution of 1917, Russia adopted a version of the song as its national anthem.

The modern anthem is based on a version arranged in 1887. Some modern French people consider the words too violent. The translation, below, is of the first verse and chorus.

Arise you children of our Fatherland / Oh now is here our glorious day! / Over us the bloodstained banner / Of tyranny holds sway.

Oh do you hear there in our fields / The roar of those fierce fighting men? / Who came right here into our midst / To slaughter sons, wives and kin!

Chorus:

To arms, oh citizens! / Form up in serried ranks! / March on, march on! / And drench our fields / With their tainted blood!

Moreover, everyone knew that his Austrian-born queen was opposed to the Revolution. Since Austria was among the ranks of France's enemies, the queen's position became ever more precarious.

The French army opposing the Austrians and Prussians was weak because thousands of French officers, who were all noblemen, had emigrated. Soldiers did not trust the officers who remained. Some units mutinied against their officers. Other units experienced widespread desertions. Overall, the poorly disciplined and poorly motivated French army was falling to pieces.

In June 1792, Prussia declared war on France. The allied Prussian and Austrian armies marched toward France. After the French army suffered a series of defeats, it became clear that the Brissotins did not know how to conduct war. For this reason, the Legislative Assembly removed the Brissotins from important government positions.

Next, the Legislative Assembly issued a dramatic statement that the "fatherland," the term they used to refer to France, was in danger. This statement authorized all government bodies to remain in permanent session so they could raise volunteers to join the army. Citizens armed themselves with whatever weapons they could find and formed local militia units. Moreover, from all over the country, volunteers converged on Paris to defend the capital. Those from France's Mediterranean seaport of Marseilles entered Paris singing a bloodthirsty battle hymn. Forever after, this hymn went by the name "the Marseillaise." It remains the modern French national anthem.

Until this point in time, only male property owners in France could vote. At the urging of a brilliant political speaker named Georges Danton, a Parisian district decided to give men who did not own property the vote. The movement spread. The combination of arming the militia and allowing all men the vote marked a radical change.

Just how radical became apparent when a Prussian commander threatened to destroy Paris if King Louis XVI was harmed. The fact that a foreign enemy army supported the French king persuaded many French citizens that Louis XVI was an enemy too. The announcement that "the fatherland was in danger" had already inflamed revolutionary spirit. The Prussian threat caused a Parisian mob to attack the royal palace on August 10, 1792. The king fled for safety to the Legislative Assembly. Meanwhile, the mob slaughtered the king's Swiss Guards (made up of four battalions of mercenaries, or professional soldiers for hire, who served as the king's bodyguards). It was the bloodiest day so far in the Revolution.

THE AFTERMATH OF THE FRENCH REVOLUTION

The Legislative Assembly responded to the general violence by voting to suspend the monarchy. It decided to hold an election for a new political unit, called the National Convention. In turn, the convention would prepare a constitution. In effect, the summer of 1792 witnessed a second revolution. Any chance for a compromise allowing the king to retain some power had disappeared. In addition, the lower-class artisans, called the sansculottes, fully participated in the revolution. (*Sansculottes* literally means "without breeches." It was a term used to describe lower-class supporters of the Revolution.) The stage was set for class conflict.

September Massacres

The French Legislative Assembly hastily organized armies to protect France's eastern frontier along the Rhine. It did the same on the northern frontier in Austrian-controlled Flanders (modern Belgium). In this crisis, radical leaders took control of the French government. The most influential was Georges Danton. Danton had the ability to energize the mob with his fiery speeches. He and his allies pushed a variety of emergency measures through the assembly. Parisian prisons filled with people suspected of opposing the government, many of whom were rounded up with little evidence of wrongdoing.

Another leader, journalist Jean-Paul Marat, emerged in a powerful position. Marat called himself the friend of the people. He argued for extreme and bloodthirsty measures. On September 2, 1792, for example, the mob broke into the Paris prisons. Over four days, the mob held its own trials of the prisoners and eventually executed about fourteen hundred prisoners, most of whom were common criminals. Since the beginning of the Revolution, executions had only occasionally taken place. The events of September 2 were different. Lawlessness and terror occurred on a much bigger scale. These events horrified people both inside and outside of France. They also marked the transfer of power from the assembly to the Parisian mob.

VALMY: A DECISIVE BATTLE

Hardly anyone thought that the allied (joint) invasion of France by Austria and Prussia could be stopped. The invading armies bypassed the fortress of Verdun in northeastern France and headed toward Paris. On September 20, 1792, about 52,000 French soldiers, a combination of professionals and inexperienced volunteers, engaged 34,000 professional soldiers belonging to the Prussian army. The encounter came at a place called Valmy in northeastern France. Rival lines of cannons traded shots, and to everyone's amazement, the French volunteers stood firm. Although about 86,000 soldiers were present, little fighting took place aside from the cannon fire. The French lost about 300 men; the Prussians had about 180 killed and wounded. Yet the inability of the Prussians to drive off the French provided an immense psychological lift to French morale.

> ## FAST FACT
>
> THE FRENCH LOST ABOUT 300 MEN AND THE PRUSSIANS HAD ABOUT 180 KILLED AND WOUNDED AT THE BATTLE OF VALMY IN 1792.

The Revolution had survived its first great foreign military challenge. Poet Wolfgang Goethe was serving in the Prussian army. The evening following the Valmy battle, he said, "From this place and this time forth commences a new era in world history." Indeed, the

THE FRENCH VICTORY AT THE BATTLE OF VALMY ON SEPTEMBER 20, 1792, WAS A TREMENDOUS BOOST TO FRENCH MORALE. THIS OIL PAINTING BY HORACE VERNET IS FROM 1826.

next day, the newly elected French National Convention voted to abolish the monarchy.

Six months of brilliant French military successes followed. The victories intoxicated revolutionary leaders. They resolved to spread revolutionary ideals throughout Europe at the point of French bayonets. "Fraternity and help to all peoples wishing to recover their liberty" was their call. French generals received instructions to impose revolutionary reforms in all conquered territories. One French politician said, "We cannot be calm until Europe, all Europe, is in flames."

CHAPTER 4

The Terror

IN PARIS THE CONVENTION DEBATED what to do with Louis XVI, eventually deciding to put him on trial. The outcome was never in doubt. The lurking presence of the Parisian mob prevented any hope of leniency. After a two-day trial, the convention voted the death sentence. On January 21, 1793, the king was executed. The execution—beheading at the guillotine—was staged as a public spectacle, attended by thousands.

While many of the spectators greeted the execution with cheers, others understood the gravity of killing a king. A lawyer who had helped prepare the king's defense reported,

> No sooner had the crime [the execution] been consummated than someone standing at the foot of the scaffold shouted "Long live the People!" and the cry was taken up on every side and swept through the whole of that vast crowd. The shouting was followed by a deep, dejected silence. Shame, horror,

fear were already hovering above the immense open space. . . .
The crowd was walking slowly, scarcely daring to look at one
another. . . . The assassins had lost their customary insolence;
confronted by the public grief, they were speechless."

CIVIL WAR COMES TO FRANCE

The execution of Louis XVI convinced Great Britain and the Dutch
Republic (modern-day Netherlands) to enter the war against revolutionary France. Soon Spain and several Italian states joined in.
The convention responded by ordering the conscription (military
draft) of three hundred thousand more soldiers. This order led to
civil war inside of France when certain areas of the country refused
to provide the men. Pockets of France that still supported the
monarchy rebelled.

*"The assassins [the king's executioners] had lost
their customary insolence; confronted by the public
grief, they were speechless."*

—a lawyer for King Louis XVI, 1793

In addition, the Revolution's attack against the Catholic Church
had offended many people. Priests urged the people to resist the government. So, areas with deep religious ties formed their own fighting
units. These guerrilla units (fighters who do not belong to a regular, organized, uniformed army) fought against the Revolution. A
religious-based movement against the Revolution was centered in the

Vendée, a region south of France's Loire River. The Vendée witnessed bitter, brutal fighting until the rebels were eventually crushed.

Elsewhere on the military front, the year 1793 saw the European allies drive French forces out of the Rhineland and Belgium. After the defeat of his forces, one French commander, General Charles Dumouriez, deserted to the Austrians. On the French home front, food prices rose, and the value of the assignat (France's revolutionary currency) fell even more. Food riots erupted again in Paris.

These setbacks brought to a head the political divisions within the convention. The Girondins argued that the convention must ignore the influence of the Parisian mob. The revolutionary faction led by Maximilien Robespierre, called the Montagnards (literally "mountain men" because they sat in ranks at the highest point in the assembly hall), disagreed. The Montagnards feared the sansculottes and believed it too dangerous to oppose them. They also thought that they could not control events without the help of the sansculottes.

The Montagnards and the Jacobins encouraged a popular revolt against the bourgeois Girondins. It was easy to provoke the poorer classes to attack the Girondins. A three-day revolt in Paris that began on May 31, 1793, featured both the sansculottes and another, even more radical group called the Enragés (the Enraged). The Enragés were extreme revolutionaries who advocated the common ownership of goods and strict economic controls.

When the sansculottes and the Enragés demanded the expulsion of the Girondins from the convention, the Montagnards agreed. Twenty-nine Girondin delegates went to prison. Other Girondins returned to the countryside to encourage opposition to the Montagnards. The political fighting was causing the Revolution to turn inward upon itself.

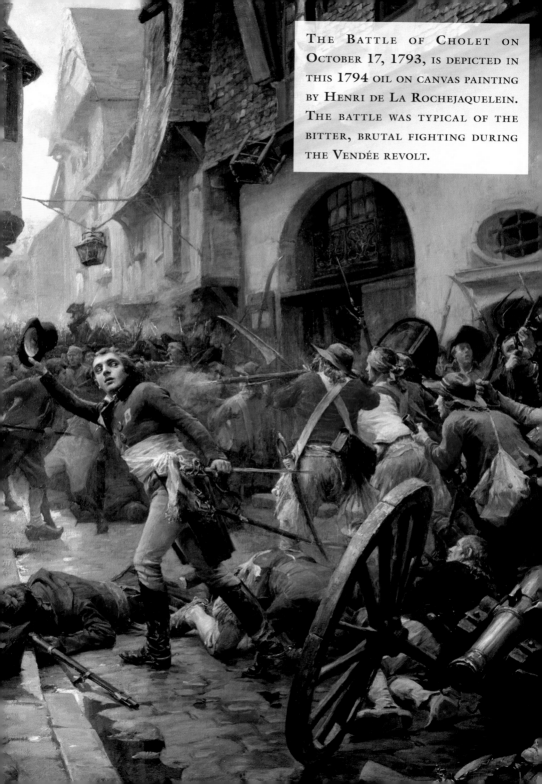

THE BATTLE OF CHOLET ON OCTOBER 17, 1793, IS DEPICTED IN THIS 1794 OIL ON CANVAS PAINTING BY HENRI DE LA ROCHEJAQUELEIN. THE BATTLE WAS TYPICAL OF THE BITTER, BRUTAL FIGHTING DURING THE VENDÉE REVOLT.

A prominent example of this inward trend occurred on July 13, 1793. A young woman named Charlotte Corday strongly supported the Girondins. She had attended Girondin meetings and become convinced that the politician Jean-Paul Marat was to blame for the fall of the Girondins. She traveled to Paris, where she assassinated Marat while he was in his bathtub. During her subsequent trial, she explained her motive: she had wanted to kill "a wild beast who was devouring all Frenchmen." Marat's assassination was a sign of the times. Much worse was to follow.

The Short Life of Charlotte Corday

A CONVENT-EDUCATED twenty-four-year-old, Marie-Anne-Charlotte Corday D'Armont lived in Caen in western France. She was from a poor but aristocratic family and lived a quiet life. Corday became involved in revolutionary politics when Caen became the refuge of a group of Girondins who had fled Paris. She became convinced that Jean-Paul Marat was responsible for the execution of hundreds during the September 1792 massacre, and she hatched a solitary plan to kill him.

Corday went to Paris on July 9, 1793. There she bought a knife, took a hotel room, and wrote a statement explaining why she planned to kill Marat. Pretending that she had important information about Marat's enemies, Corday made several requests to see him before she was allowed to meet him in his bath on July 13. (Marat often conducted business in his bath because he suffered from a painful skin condition.) Corday gave him the names of enemies, whom he promised to send to the guillotine. Then she drew out the concealed knife and stabbed him in the heart.

As was typical during this period of the Revolution, Charlotte Corday went to trial only three days after the killing and went calmly to the guillotine the next day, July 17. As a result of her act, revolutionary sympathizers in France and elsewhere elevated Marat to the status of a martyr.

THE DEATH OF MARAT AT THE HANDS OF CHARLOTTE CORDAY IS
DEPICTED IN JACQUES-LOUIS DAVID'S 1793 OIL PAINTING.

The Girondins had not been alone in their dislike of the influence of the Parisian mob. Many people throughout France had always resented Parisian influence. Now they had additional reasons to dislike Paris: they blamed the sansculottes for the prevailing political and economic instability. In the summer of 1793, several cities in the outlying provinces of France, including Bordeaux,

Lazare Carnot: "Organizer of Victory"

During the early years of the French Revolution, the French armies confronted enormous problems. More than any other person, Lazare Carnot helped prevent defeat of the French armies. Carnot was a key member of government, with special responsibility for military matters. He made two enormous contributions. He created the French program of national conscription (a military draft), called the *levée en masse*, or mass conscription. He also created the *députés-en-mission* system (special delegates holding extraordinary powers). For these crucial contributions, Carnot became celebrated as the "Organizer of Victory."

the home of the Girondins, revolted. The manufacturing city of Lyon and the prominent port city of Marseilles also revolted. In August the great port of Toulon rebelled and admitted the British navy into its harbor. This was treachery on a big scale against the Revolution.

Although much of France was in revolt against the convention, the rebels were unable to coordinate their efforts. During the autumn, convention forces methodically suppressed the rebels. Special courts sentenced about fourteen thousand rebels to death. Some were killed by firing squads or drowning. Most died beneath the blade of the guillotine.

Meanwhile, in Paris the Montagnards showed themselves unable to organize a government. Without firm direction, the sansculottes dominated decision making. The needs and hatreds of the mob controlled events. Two important legislative measures arose from this period. On August 23, 1793, the government declared mass conscription (levée en masse). This was an unprecedented appeal to an entire nation to mobilize for war.

COMMITTEE OF PUBLIC SAFETY

The government took this action through its Committee of Public Safety. The National Convention had formed this committee just a few months earlier, in March 1793. It directly supervised the military and possessed the power to take anything from anybody in order to support the war. As time passed, this committee became ever more powerful. It acted as it saw fit and was ready to act outside of legal bounds in order to defend the republic.

> *"From this moment until that in which the enemy shall have been driven from the soil of the Republic, all Frenchmen are in permanent requisition for the service of the armies."*
>
> —proclamation by the Committee of Public Safety, 1793

The Committee of Public Safety issued a proclamation with its August 23 order for the levée en masse.

From this moment until that in which the enemy shall have been driven from the soil of the Republic, all Frenchmen are in permanent requisition for the service of the armies. The young men shall go to battle; the married men shall forge arms and transport provisions; the women shall make tents and clothing and shall serve in the hospitals; the children shall turn old linen into lint [for bandages]; the aged shall betake themselves to the public places in order to arouse the courage of the warriors and preach the hatred of the kings and the unity of the Republic.

THE COMMITTEE OF PUBLIC SAFETY WAS FORMED IN 1793 BY THE NATIONAL CONVENTION TO OVERSEE THE DEFENSE OF THE FRENCH REPUBLIC.

Immediately, all young men between the ages of eighteen and twenty-five received orders to assemble for military drill. Farmers received orders to provide food for them. To shelter the soldiers, church property became national buildings to be used as barracks. During the next year, the mass conscription law raised more than three-quarters of a million conscripts. It provided the republic with the manpower to resist its foreign enemies.

The patriotic French citizen-soldier was different from his European foes. Instead of fighting for a monarch or a privileged class, as were most European soldiers, he was fighting for a nation. Moreover, he felt that he had a personal stake in that nation. This change marked the beginning of nationalism (strong loyalty to a nation). And it would influence the actions and views of people in other countries around the world.

The levée en masse successfully focused the nation on the war effort. On the home front, new factories produced weapons and gunpowder. Within the army, the officer corps no longer contained antirevolutionary men. A new set of skilled, tough officers arose. Among the rank and file, the soldiers were brave and patriotic. The discipline of the old army had been blended with the enthusiasm of the new conscripts to create an imposing fighting force. During 1794 the republican army won notable victories.

On the downside, mass conscription also triggered widespread resistance to the draft. In the French regions of Brittany and western Normandy, for example, draft evaders joined a guerrilla group called the *chouans* (antirevolutionary fighters) whose goal was to protect traditional community norms against new republican values. The chouans also advocated the return of the dead king's son to the throne of France. The battle between the revolutionary government and the chouans grew into a small civil war. It drained valuable resources away from the war with foreign enemies.

The army faced other huge problems. It was still hard to fill the army's basic needs. Uniforms were poorly made and quickly wore out. The new muskets quickly rusted or broke because of a lack of cleaning materials, oil, and grease. Too often soldiers went hungry. And those who were wounded or ill got little care.

FAST FACT

IN 1794 THE MASS CONSCRIPTION LAW RAISED MORE THAN THREE-QUARTERS OF A MILLION CONSCRIPTS (SOLDIERS), PROVIDING THE REPUBLIC WITH THE MANPOWER TO RESIST ITS FOREIGN ENEMIES.

The Revolutionary Army in Battle

NATIONAL CONSCRIPTION, the levée en masse, drafted thousands of men into the ranks of the French army. Although the conscripts were not highly trained, they fought with enormous patriotic enthusiasm. A French officer wrote this description which, while painting a romanticized picture, captures the spirit of a typical engagement in the revolutionary period:

> Once the chink in the foe's armour had been revealed, it became the focal point for the main effort. . . . Then, when the hail of enemy bullets or cannon balls began to slacken, an officer, common soldier, or as often as not, a Representative of the People [a deputy-on-mission] would start to chant the "Hymn of Victory" [the Marseillaise]. The general would place his hat with its large tricolor cockade on the point of his sword so that it could be seen from afar and serve as a rallying point for the gallant troops. The soldiers would begin to run forwards . . . as the drums beat the charge; the sky would ring to a thousand battle-cries constantly repeated: "En avant! En avant! [Forward!] Vive la République! [Long live the Republic!]"

The French navy was in worse shape. The experienced naval leaders had all been members of the nobility. They had either fled France or been executed. Their replacements had no experience in the complex craft of maneuvering battle fleets. So, when a French fleet went to battle against Britain at sea in May 1794, it stood little chance against the well-trained, experienced British navy. The result of this battle became known as "The Glorious First of June," a great British naval victory.

GOVERNMENT BY DECREE

The National Convention had declared repeatedly that it represented the French people. During this time of turmoil, the convention

THE AFTERMATH OF THE FRENCH REVOLUTION

was supposed to write a constitution. For nine months, delegates did labor at writing a constitution while governing the country by decree (orders). Many of the decrees called for special powers far beyond legal boundaries. Then, when the delegates finished writing the constitution of 1793, the convention immediately suspended its implementation. For two more years, the convention governed by decree, transforming France. The convention laid the foundation for a French republic that endures today.

But in the fall of 1793, most delegates (the elected officials called deputies) were concerned with restoring order and defeating the rebels. Rumors of conspiracy circulated. It seemed to the revolutionary leaders that they were surrounded by treachery. These events strengthened the hands of the radicals so that the bloody-minded Parisian mob was able to continue its influence over the convention. Not understanding why affairs were going so poorly, the sansculottes demanded ever harsher steps.

A mass demonstration on September 5, 1793, caused the Legislative Assembly to adopt a new policy. One spokesman explained: "It is time that equality bore its scythe above all heads. It is time to horrify the conspirators. So legislators, place Terror on the order of the day! Let us be in revolution, because everywhere counter-revolution is being roven [spun] by our enemies. The blade of the law should hover over all the guilty."

> # FAST FACT
>
> AN ESTIMATED 20,000 PEOPLE, MOSTLY PEASANTS AND WORKING PEOPLE, WERE EXECUTED DURING THE REIGN OF TERROR.

THE TERROR BEGINS

And so began the Reign of Terror. The Jacobins became the dominant political faction. They took charge of the government by controlling the Committee on Public Safety and the Committee on General Security. In turn, these committees created special tribunals, or courts, and special committees. The objective was to eliminate all possible enemies of the people. At first, the Terror was intended to locate and kill traitors in a time of war. As time passed, the men in power used the Terror to kill political rivals. No one was safe during the Reign of Terror. Men and women, rich and poor, high-ranking politician, lowest criminal—all could be swept up by authorities and executed. In his memoirs, a French politician recalled that the Terror brought "its bloody scepter to the entire nation."

Meanwhile, new decrees imposed price controls on all basic goods such as food. A "Maximum" set a top, or maximum price. Some deputies saw this as the beginning of a new economic order. One young radical leader, Louis Saint-Just, argued that there should neither be rich nor poor. To accomplish this, the government passed laws to limit inheritance and to sell national properties to poor people. To enforce its decrees, the convention sent special agents, called representatives-on-mission throughout the country.

The majority of the French living during the Terror feared the sudden arrival of these government representatives who had the power to uproot their lives. The representatives-on-mission could replace all local officials, who immediately became suspects and were placed under house arrest or thrown in prison. The representatives could alter community relations however they saw fit. They enjoyed great power and were much feared.

Revolutionary tribunals were authorized to arrest people suspected of opposing the Revolution. The convention passed a "Law of Suspects" on September 17, 1793. All ex-nobles, including women and children, faced arrest unless they could prove that they supported the Revolution. Anyone who had criticized the Revolution also faced

FRENCH ARISTOCRATS WAIT TO BE SUMMONED TO EXECUTION BY GUILLOTINE IN 1793. THIS OIL PAINTING DATES TO THE EIGHTEENTH CENTURY.

arrest. Surveillance committees sprang up throughout the country to enforce the Law of Suspects. The Law of Suspects was a broad law. Likewise, the surveillance committees enjoyed broad powers. Thus, a legal system open to abuse and in which neighbor could turn on neighbor was created.

In the words of one historian, in Paris during the Terror "there was to be literally no excuse for not being an ardent patriot." Anyone could denounce someone they did not like, leading to that person's arrest. Within a year, about three hundred thousand people were arrested under the Law of Suspects. In the name of law, terrible crimes were committed.

On October 10, 1793, the government declared it would employ revolutionary measures until peace came. In its earliest days, the Revolution had sought to govern within constitutional boundaries. Now terror became a fundamental principle of the revolutionary government. The revolutionary army was to carry the Terror throughout the republic.

DECHRISTIANISATION

The year 1793 witnessed an accelerating attack by revolutionary leaders against the Catholic Church. One of these leaders was a former priest named Joseph Fouché. Fouché believed that Christianity could not exist alongside the Revolution. He particularly disliked clerical vows of celibacy. So, he ordered clerics who refused to marry to adopt and support orphans or aged people. He also issued a manifesto, a public declaration or edict, that recognized no religion except what he called universal morality. These acts against the church were the beginning of "dechristianisation," an effort to create a secular (nonreligious) society in France. The Declaration of the Rights of Man and Citizen had provided for religious freedom. Fouché wanted to ensure that such freedom was driven underground (not exercised in public).

A symbol of the attack against religion was the creation of a new calendar. Revolutionary leaders decided that this new revolutionary calendar would begin with 1792, the first year of the French Republic, instead of with the birth of Christ. The word "Saint" began to be removed from street names. Revolutionary leaders renamed the great cathedral of Notre Dame in Paris "the Temple of Reason." Parisian leaders banned clerical dress among church staff. Toward the end of 1793, the city's leaders closed all churches in Paris. The closing of churches in the rest of France soon followed. In effect, the French government was trying to stamp out the practice of traditional religion.

Dechristianisation became a growing part of the Terror. Within France, areas that had rebelled against the revolutionary government saw their churches vandalized. The convention decreed that any priest who was denounced by six citizens was subject to deportation (being

sent out of the country). By the spring of 1794, dechristianisation reached its peak. Except for very remote areas, no church was open for public worship. Outside of France, churches became the special target for looting by the French army.

THE TERROR CONTINUES

In the autumn of 1793 came revenge trials, most famously against France's ex-queen, the hated Marie Antoinette. A grim roll call of the condemned began: October 16, Marie Antoinette executed; October 31, the Girondin leaders executed; November 6, the Duke of Orléans—the king's cousin and a man who had renounced his noble birth and taken the name Philippe Égalité (equality)—executed; November 8, Madame Roland, a prominent socialite whose crime was befriending the wrong people, executed.

The city of Lyon had again rebelled against the revolutionary government. The government sent its forces to enforce its will and make an example of the city. Its representative-on-mission published a directive to the local revolutionary leaders that began, "The goal of the Revolution is the happiness of the People." It then authorized the use of Terror without limit because, "For those who act in the sense of the revolution, everything is permissible."

The leader of the revolutionary forces reported to the Committee of Public Safety that among Lyon's 120,000 inhabitants were only 1,500 guilt-free men. Arrests and executions followed. When Fouché concluded that the executions were going too slowly, he tried to kill in batches. Sixty men were chained together and blasted with cannon fire. The next day, 211 men faced the same death. Fouché reported to Paris, "The butchery has been good." In the coming months, more than 1,800 citizens were executed and the wealthiest sections of Lyon destroyed.

The Revolutionary Calendar

FRANCE ADOPTED THE revolutionary calendar in 1793 to mark its complete break with the old order and declare its difference from the rest of the world. The new calendar began with the date September 22, 1792—the day France was proclaimed a republic, and the first day of autumn— calling that day 1 Vendémiaire, year I. Each of the new months had thirty days, divided into three ten-day weeks called "décades." The names of the months were coined from Latin, French, or Greek roots reflecting the natural world during the changing seasons. The three months of each season had the same suffix (-aire, -ôse, -al, -or). The five extra days (six in leap years), each with its own name, fell at the end of the year, September 17–21. The calendar remained in use until it was abolished in 1805.

Along with the new calendar came a new system of timekeeping. Each day was divided into ten hours, each with one hundred minutes, which were in turn divided into one hundred seconds. Thus, each new hour was equivalent to more than two traditional hours. The new clocks were not widely accepted, and most users abandoned them within a couple of years.

Vendémiaire (vintage)	September/October
Brumaire (mist)	October/November
Frimaire (frost)	November/December
Nivôse (snow)	December/January
Pluviôse (rain)	January/February
Ventôse (wind)	February/March
Germinal (seed)	March/April
Floréal (flower)	April/May
Prairial (meadow)	May/June
Messidor (harvest)	June/July
Thermidor (heat)	July/August
Fructidor (fruit)	August/September

The Guillotine

THE GUILLOTINE WAS introduced in France in 1792 by the French physician and politician Joseph-Ignace Guillotin. With fellow physician Antoine Louis, he oversaw the fabrication of a mechanical device with a heavy blade, held in place by two grooved posts. The device was thought to guarantee a quick and relatively painless death. A similar machine had already been used in Great Britain and in Europe to execute condemned nobles. As a member of the National Assembly, Guillotin proposed a law requiring that all executions be carried out by such a machine. Previously, only those of noble birth were decapitated, while more lowly convicts were executed by hanging. The first execution by guillotine in France occurred in 1792 and the last in 1977. France abolished capital punishment in 1981.

IN THIS EIGHTEENTH-CENTURY ENGRAVING, DR. JOSEPH-IGNACE GUILLOTIN, WITH SWORD, DEMONSTRATES THE EFFECTIVENESS OF HIS INVENTION—THE GUILLOTINE.

During the Reign of Terror, an estimated 20,000 people were executed. Only about 15 percent of the victims belonged to the clergy or nobility. The balance were peasants and working people—the very people in whose name the Revolution had begun.

CHAPTER 5

"A Frightful Mess"

A S 1793 CAME TO AN END, it appeared that the Terror had successfully crushed internal opposition. Thousands of recruits, summoned by the levée en masse, had reinforced the armies. The armies, in turn, again started to win battles. One notable success came in December 1793, when the army drove the British out of Toulon. Here, an obscure, twenty-four-year-old artillery captain named Napoléon Bonaparte rose to fame. He planned and executed a successful attack that forced the British to evacuate Toulon. The government responded by promoting him to brigadier general. The recapture of Toulon proved the first step in the career of one of history's most brilliant military commanders.

By the spring of 1794, French armies had recaptured all of the republic's territory. Consequently, some politicians began to argue for the end to the Terror. In response, a group of popular leaders, called the Hébertists (taken from the name of Jacques Hébert, a spokesman for the mob) tried to silence the critics of the Terror. The Hébertists mounted a coup (sudden overthrow of the government). The Committee of Public Safety outmaneuvered the Hébertists and sent them to the guillotine. It was one more sign of the Revolution turning on itself.

EXECUTION OF DANTON

In their scramble for power, the representatives-on-mission began attacking one another. It was up to the Committee of Public Safety to sort out these attacks. Danton became a voice of religious toleration and political moderation: "We must pursue traitors everywhere, whatever their disguise, but we must be careful to distinguish between error and crime." Alarmed by the course of events, Danton concluded: "Perhaps the Terror once served a useful purpose, but

> *"No one wants to see a person treated as a criminal just because he happens not to have enough revolutionary enthusiasm."*
>
> —Georges Danton, 1794

it should not hurt innocent people. No one wants to see a person treated as a criminal just because he happens not to have enough revolutionary enthusiasm."

Such talk put Danton at odds with many deputies. Radical leader Saint-Just disagreed strongly with Danton. "A man is guilty of crime against the Republic," Saint-Just said, "when he takes pity on prisoners. . . . He is guilty because he is opposed to the Terror."

Eyewitness to Execution

AN EYEWITNESS DESCRIBED the execution of a duchess and her family:

> The carts [carrying the condemned] halted before the scaffold. . . . There was a large circle of spectators, most of them laughing, "There she is ! Look at her!" . . . When all is ready the old man goes up the steps. The chief executioner takes him by the left arm, the big assistant by the right, and the other by the legs. They lay him quickly on his face and his head is cut off and thrown, together with his body, into a great tumbril [cart], where all the bodies swim in blood. And so it goes on. . . . The Duchess is the third to go up. They have to make an opening in the top of her dress to uncover her neck. Her daughter-in-law is the tenth. . . . The chief executioner tears off her bonnet. It is fastened by a pin so her hair is pulled violently upwards and she grimaces with pain. When the daughter-in-law is gone the grand-daughter replaces her."

By now, the revolutionary leadership had split into factions. Maximilien Robespierre was the dominant voice on the Committee of Public Safety. He was known as an honest man, the "Incorruptible Robespierre." But his specialty was politics, and he was not skilled or practical in running a government. His basic idea about diplomacy, for example, was to see everything through the lens of foreign plotters. It made for good political theater to blame setbacks on outside conspiracy and treachery. It also distracted attention from the real failures of the Committee of Public Safety. Likewise, in military affairs, Robespierre had little notion of strategy. When a French army lost a battle, his response was to guillotine the commanding general. Lastly, he was deeply ignorant about economics.

Robespierre's failings were widely known within the Committee of Public Safety. One colleague wrote that he "never had the faintest idea about government, administration, and diplomacy." Danton spoke about his total lack of practicality by saying that Robespierre "couldn't even boil an egg." But Robespierre knew how to use the tools of terror to eliminate his foes.

He became suspicious of both Danton and Danton's friends. When someone warned Danton that Robespierre was plotting his

AN ENGRAVING FROM THE 1800S BY C. H. BARBART DEPICTS GEORGES DANTON, CENTER, JUST BEFORE HIS EXECUTION ON APRIL 5, 1794.

destruction, Danton was amazed. He crudely replied, "If I thought he had the slightest idea of this kind, I will devour his intestines." Robespierre caused Danton to be denounced and executed on April 5, 1794.

Danton met his fate bravely. He said "I'm leaving everything in a frightful mess." Referring to the members of the Committee of Public Safety, he observed, "There's not one of them who knows anything about government." An eyewitness recorded Danton's final words as he mounted the guillotine: "Danton was the last to appear on the platform, soaked with the blood of his friends. . . . I recall the full force of my feeling at Danton's last words . . . which were passed round with horror and admiration: 'Above all, don't forget to show my head to the people: it's worth seeing.'"

THE GREAT TERROR

Danton's execution marked another acceleration of the Terror. The Committee of Public Safety passed harsher laws, including a notorious law on June 10, 1794, called the Law of 22 Prairial (a date on the revolutionary calendar). The Law of 22 Prairial removed the last judicial safeguards protecting a person's innocence so that the only allowable punishment for so-called public enemies was death. A revolutionary tribunal acted as the court, but before this court, the odds were hopelessly stacked against the defendant (the accused person). The defendant could neither use a lawyer nor summon witnesses for his defense. A supporter of the Law of 22 Prairial explained, "For a citizen to become suspect it is sufficient that rumour accuses him."

The ensuing weeks of arrests and executions became known as the "Great Terror." No one felt safe because the government had defined political crimes so broadly that it was easy to make accusations that led to arrest. People were arrested merely on the basis of what they might do rather than what they had done. The Great Terror struck particularly hard at the remaining nobles.

> *"Terror is nothing other than justice, prompt, severe, inflexible; it is therefore an emanation [outgrowth] of virtue."*
>
> —Robespierre, 1794

Robespierre justified the Terror in a speech to the National Convention: "We have not been too severe. . . . Without the revolutionary Government the Republic cannot be made stronger." In another speech in February 1794, he said, "Terror is nothing other than justice, prompt, severe, inflexible; it is therefore an emanation [outgrowth] of virtue." The "incorruptible" Robespierre probably truly believed what he said. But he also knew that only the force of the Terror was keeping him in power.

ROBESPIERRE'S FALL AND EXECUTION

No one knew how the Reign of Terror could end. If someone merely criticized the government, that person faced execution. A politician who survived the Terror recalled, "For the friends of liberty, the terror was more devastating than for its enemies. The latter [nobles] had emigrated." Those who remained "dutiful and patriotic" were "consumed" by the Terror. Yet, by July 1794, people had to wonder why the Terror continued. Inside France, antirevolutionary rebels had been crushed and foreign armies driven from French soil. Indeed,

French armies were now carrying the fight to enemy soil. People began to blame Robespierre for unnecessarily continuing the Terror.

Deputies in the convention feared that Robespierre would start to target them. They met secretly to arrange his overthrow. Robespierre's enemies successfully bested him in a memorable confrontation on July 26, 1794, during a debate in the halls of the convention. They literally shouted him down. The next day, Robespierre appealed to his former allies, the sansculottes and the Jacobin Club. The Jacobins had previously acknowledged Robespierre as their leader. On this dramatic day, neither the sansculottes nor the Jacobins rallied to support Robespierre.

The convention outlawed Robespierre. This meant that when authorities arrested Robespierre, there was no need for a trial. On

A 1794 LITHOGRAPH BY M. MELINQUE DEPICTS A WOUNDED ROBESPIERRE, ON TABLE. HE WAS ARRESTED BY THE CONVENTION ON JULY 27, 1794, AND CONDEMNED WITHOUT TRIAL.

July 28, Robespierre and his closest followers were executed by guillotine. On the same day, the convention repealed the notorious Law of 22 Prairial. The next day, another seventy-one members of Robespierre's faction were executed, the most people killed in one day by the guillotine in Paris.

THE END OF THE TERROR

Robespierre's execution marked the end of the Terror. A Parisian observed the relief and joy Robespierre's death produced: "People were embracing each other in the streets; they were so surprised to be still among the living that their rejoicing turned almost into madness." Revenge killings and public executions continued the following year but not in the savage numbers of the previous year. The most radical and violent phase of the Revolution was over.

> **FAST FACT**
>
> SEVENTY-ONE MEMBERS OF ROBESPIERRE'S FACTION WERE EXECUTED ON JULY 29, 1794—THE MOST PEOPLE KILLED IN ONE DAY BY THE GUILLOTINE IN PARIS.

Many of the Terror laws were either repealed or significantly loosened. After August 5, 1794, vague suspicion was no longer enough to arrest a suspect; instead there had to be specific charges. Five days later, the power of the revolutionary tribunal was restricted. Henceforth, guilt had to be proven with clear evidence of counterrevolutionary intent. That same month, more than thirty-five hundred suspects were released from Parisian jails.

At the same time, former leaders of the Terror scrambled to escape blame. The famous Swiss writer Anne-Louise-Germaine de Staël lived during these times. She cynically described the conduct of former leaders of the Terror: "The apologies of those who had shared in the reign of terror formed truly the most inconceivable school of sophistry [reasoning that on the surface seems correct but is actually faulty]. . . . Some said that they had been constrained [forced] to whatever they had done . . . others pretended that they had sacrificed themselves to the public good, though it was known that they had thought only on self-preservation." Madame de Staël concluded with disgust that everyone was heaping blame upon easy targets in order to avoid taking

ROBESPIERRE AND HIS SUPPORTERS ARE LED TO THE GUILLOTINE FOR EXECUTION ON JULY 28, 1794, IN THIS NINETEENTH-CENTURY OIL PAINTING BY ALFRED FRANÇOIS MOUILLARD.

personal responsibility. However, the Revolution was not over. The issues that had caused division and conflict—the legitimacy of the monarchy, the role of privilege, the role of religion, and the desire to spread revolutionary ideals via war—remained. In addition, the Jacobins had become increasingly powerful and more radical. Controlling the Jacobins became an ever-more urgent problem.

FAST FACT

BY THE MID-1790S, THE GAP BETWEEN RICH AND POOR WAS ALMOST AS WIDE AS IT HAD BEEN BEFORE THE REVOLUTION.

New leaders arose in the convention to replace Robespierre's faction. They were called the Thermidoreans, named for the month in the revolutionary calendar when Robespierre had been executed. The Thermidoreans set to work destroying the Jacobins and their work. Some of their measures were popular. However, the agricultural harvest in the fall of 1794 was poor and the following winter very cold. The national currency, the assignat, fell in value by more than 90 percent. Food prices soared. By spring, the suffering sansculottes blamed the government. To them it seemed that all the progress made during the Revolution was being undone. The gap between rich and poor was almost as wide as it had been before the Revolution.

Consequently, an angry Parisian mob twice stormed the convention and even managed to lynch (hang) a deputy. However, for the first time since the Revolution had begun, the government decided it possessed enough strength to fight back against the sansculottes. It was able to summon the National Guard to oppose the sansculottes. Together, the convention and the National Guard defeated the sansculottes, ending the influence of the Parisian mob for the next two generations.

The convention then began to react to the excesses of the Revolution and the Terror. Churches were allowed to reopen. The ruthless effort to depopulate the Vendée, the former home of antigovernment rebels, ended. There was even talk of restoring the monarchy.

Such talk helped encourage French royalists to prepare a comeback. When the young son of the executed King Louis XVI died of natural causes, the boy's uncle (brother of Louis XVI) proclaimed himself Louis XVIII. Louis XVIII did not dare return, but other lesser-ranking royalists received British assistance and invaded Brittany in northwestern France. They hoped to encourage the local population—who in the past had shown strong support for the king—to form an army and march on Paris. Their effort failed miserably.

A NEW CONSTITUTION

Meanwhile, the convention drew up another constitution in 1795. It included a new declaration of the rights and duties of citizens. The first declaration had spoken about equality. Many people had interpreted this to mean economic equality, or egalitarianism. Yet experience had shown how difficult it was to create economic equality. A nobleman addressed the convention on this point when he introduced the draft of the new constitution: "At last you must guarantee the property rights of the rich . . . equality of the law is all a reasonable man can ask for. Absolute equality is a chimera [illusion]; in order to make it possible, there would have to be total equality of intellect, virtue, physical strength, education, and even of possessions of all men." By 1795 the convention decided that equality meant equality before the law, not economic equality.

This decision displeased some leaders. One writer issued a ringing challenge: "We shall determine the limits of property rights. We shall

Factions in Revolutionary France

FACTIONALISM CONVULSED French politics during the Revolution. Delegates to the various national legislatures of revolutionary France associated themselves with Parisian clubs based on political beliefs. Meanwhile, other groups formed in the countryside and—sometimes violently—pursued their political agendas. Below is a list of the main revolutionary groups.

Brissotins: This group was named for Jacques-Pierre Brissot, a Parisian journalist who served in the Legislative Assembly and supported the revolutionary wars. Many Brissotins in the assembly were well-to-do merchants from Bordeaux. Their faction was active from 1791 to 1792. They lost power after a series of military defeats led many to believe they were botching the war effort.

chouans: This band of rural guerrilla fighters battled the Revolution in northwestern France. They sympathized with the royalists but also wanted to avoid being drafted.

Cordeliers: This group of Parisian radicals formed a club in 1790. They sought to limit the abuse of power and supported the principle of the rights of man. They disbanded in 1794.

Enragés: These Parisian extremists had a brief period of influence in 1793. They sought government control of the economy and communal ownership.

Feuillants: After splintering from the Jacobins in 1789, this group pushed for a constitutional monarchy. It disbanded in 1791. The group's name came from the name of the hall where it held its meetings.

prove that the land and the soil do not belong to individuals, but to all." Another writer spoke to the French people and said that they had lived throughout history "in slavery." The Revolution had promised equality but failed to deliver: "Therefore, we demand that from now on we should live and die as equals, as we were born equals. We want real equality, or death. And we shall have this real equality, whatever the cost."

The constitution of 1795 was an attempt to use checks and balances to create a better government. It created two chambers—the

Girondins: This politically moderate group held sway in the government through 1792. They were purged from the government in June 1793 by the radical factions, and their leaders were executed later that year. The group is named for the Gironde river valley that runs through Bordeaux, the home of its leaders.

Hébertists: This group is named after Jacques Hébert, the leader of a mob that wanted to keep the Terror going. They mounted a coup in 1794 because people in government were beginning to question the Terror. The coup failed and its leaders were executed.

Jacobins: This was the most powerful political organization in revolutionary France. It consisted of a nationwide network of clubs formed by members of the National Assembly. It dominated radical politics and presided over the Terror. It lost influence in 1794 after the Terror ended.

Montagnards: These were radical members of the convention closely allied with the Jacobins.

royalists: They called for the return of the monarch to France.

sansculottes: The name of this group literally means "without breeches." Knee-length breeches were worn by men of the nobility, while working-class men wore long trousers. Sansculottes first referred to working-class revolutionaries, then came to refer to radicals in general.

Thermidoreans: This group overthrew Robespierre and the radical factions in July 1794, ending the Terror. The group is named after Thermidor, the month in the revolutionary calendar in which Robespierre was executed.

Council of Ancients with 250 members, and the Council of 500, with 500 members. The Council of 500 proposed new laws and the Ancients decided whether to accept these proposals. The Council of 500 submitted a list of candidates to the Ancients and the Ancients chose five directors from this list. This new five-man leadership group was called the Directory.

Each year one director and one-third of the members of each council had to retire so new leaders could emerge. However, to ensure their own place in the new government, the framers of the constitution of 1795 insisted that two-thirds of the delegates to the new legislative councils come from their own ranks.

Royalists had hoped that they might return to power if the elections were truly free and open to all. Instead, when they learned of the two-thirds rule, they prepared a mass protest in Paris. In response, on October 5, 1795, a member of the Directory, Paul Barras, enlisted an artillery officer named Napoléon Bonaparte to oppose the proroyalist mob.

Bonaparte had first come to prominence when he directed the successful attack against the British at Toulon back in 1793. Since that time, his career had gone nowhere. He was seriously planning to seek employment in Turkey when Barras summoned him. "Will you serve me?" Barras demanded. "You have three minutes to decide." Bonaparte quickly agreed to support the Directory against the mob. He summoned artillery and positioned it to fire at the mob. When the mob surged toward the guns, Barras gave the order and Bonaparte's artillery opened fire at point-blank range. About two hundred Parisians died before the mob dispersed. This affair again brought Bonaparte to the favorable attention of authorities.

At Toulon, Bonaparte had displayed his military skill. In the streets of Paris, he proved to the Directory his political reliability. Although no one realized it at the time, Bonaparte's actions against the mob were another decisive step toward his eventual leadership of the French government. At the time, the Directory rewarded him by appointing him to an army command. Napoléon Bonaparte took charge of a French army, called the Army of Italy, that was fighting the Austrians along Italy's Mediterranean coast. There he led the Army of Italy to brilliant victories and established his military reputation throughout Europe.

CHAPTER 6

The Directory Takes Over

THE DIRECTORY TOOK CONTROL of France at a time when the French armies were winning victories. The French had seized Belgium from the Austrians and made it part of France. They had invaded the Dutch republic and forced its surrender. Prussia and Spain made peace with France and withdrew from the coalition (group of allied nations) opposed to revolutionary France. When 1795 ended, only Austria and Great Britain remained to fight France.

PLANS TURNED UPSIDE DOWN

France's war plan for 1796 envisioned a decisive effort to drive Austria out of the war. Two French armies would advance from Germany toward Vienna. A third supporting army, the Army of Italy, would tie down Austrian forces in northern Italy. General Napoléon Bonaparte turned these plans upside down.

Bonaparte found the Army of Italy hungry, poorly uniformed, and discouraged. Royalist agents had encouraged mutiny among some regiments. The army's generals were suspicious of their new young leader. He was not yet twenty-seven years old and, in their minds, seemed to have earned his position because of his political connections rather than on merit. In spite of their skepticism, Bonaparte immediately impressed them. A general recalled the new general's first conference: "He questioned us on the position of our divisions, on the spirit and effective forces of each corps, prescribed the course we were to follow, announced that he would hold an inspection on the morrow, and on the following day attack the enemy."

Bonaparte proceeded to conduct a brilliant campaign that transformed Italy into the main theater of war. A difficult year-long series of battles brought Austria to the conference table to negotiate a peace. Great Britain remained alone to fight France.

As commander of the Army of Italy, Napoléon Bonaparte, center on horseback, conducted a brilliant campaign in northern Italy that forced Austria into peace negotiations. This nineteenth-century oil painting is by Felix Henri Philippoteaux.

Hopes for Better Days

For France the peace on the continent could not have come at a more welcome time. Although Great Britain remained unconquered, there was a general feeling in France that better days were at hand. Around this time, émigré Charles de Talleyrand-Périgord, who had fled to the United States to escape the dangers of the guillotine, returned to Paris. Talleyrand found society greatly changed: "What a contrast between the Paris of the [Directory] and that of the revolution! The revolutionary committees and the prisons have disappeared, instead there are dances, entertainments, fireworks. . . . The ladies of the royal court have disappeared, but their places are taken by the ladies of the newly rich."

Talleyrand's observation about the prominence of the "newly rich" was accurate. During the four years the Directory ruled France, its leaders concentrated on protecting themselves and the new rich. The new rich had made their fortunes during the chaos of the Terror. Often it had been a simple matter of buying the confiscated properties of the Catholic Church or of royalists. One of the directors explained government policy:

"The revolution was carried out to insure liberty and equality for all while leaving the property of each inviolate [untouched]." He concluded that "all the government's powers" must aim at maintaining the rights of the property owners. The directors feared two threats that might upset the new rich: a return of the royalists, and a new revolutionary upheaval.

POWER GRAB

The directors could have taken advantage of the peace to solve a host of economic troubles. Instead, they employed the time-honored strategy of creating external incidents to distract the population's attention from internal problems. In 1798, the Directory ordered its armies to occupy Switzerland and the Papal States (the territories of central Italy over which the pope ruled from 756 to 1870). France had no right to do this. It was a straightforward grab for territory and power, and the rest of Europe did not like it.

In response to French aggression, Great Britain assembled a second coalition. Great Britain's strength was its navy. The French navy had always found it difficult to fight successfully against the royal navy. This was made worse by the absence of many senior French naval officers, who had either been executed or had fled during the Revolution. The French navy had little chance against the royal navy. Consequently, when the Directory considered how to strike at Great Britain, it did not find many attractive options.

Napoléon Bonaparte suggested an attack on Egypt. Such a blow would threaten valuable British trade routes. The Directory agreed, in part because they sensed that a popular general such as Bonaparte was a threat to their rule. They wanted him as far away as possible so that they could rule France without interference from Napoléon. In May 1798, Bonaparte and his army sailed for Egypt. They arrived there and easily defeated the forces of the Mamelukes, who controlled Egypt. However, the brilliant British naval officer, Admiral Horatio Nelson, destroyed most of the French fleet and thereby isolated the

An Uneasy Alliance

The Directory did not trust its military generals. Many royalist army officers had left France at the start of the revolution. As a result, the politicians distrusted the political loyalties of the generals. Members of the Directory also worried about the generals' personal ambitions—and with good reason. The personal ambitions of the generals had often undermined political stability. To keep the generals in check, the Directory tried to limit their power. In time, however, the Directory became dependent on its generals. This allowed Napoléon to enhance his own reputation in the government's service and, finally, at its expense.

French in Egypt. As a result, Bonaparte proceeded to fight a land campaign that eventually secured Egypt for France.

PROBLEMS SURFACE AGAIN

Meanwhile, back in Europe, internal conflict surfaced again in France. The Directory had released the Jacobins from prison. When the Jacobins again emerged as a political power, the Directory forced them back into hiding. A small group of Jacobins plotted a coup. The Directory defeated the coup, but the national mood shifted toward more conservative politics. This shift became apparent during the national elections of 1797. Many conservative and even royalist deputies won election to the legislature. The outcome was a clear statement against the convention, against Jacobinism, and most of all against the Directory.

These developments alarmed the ruling members of the Directory. They mounted their own coup in September 1797. This coup annulled election results in more than half the country, replacing more than 177 Jacobin and royalist deputies. The Directory brought back the Terror laws so that anyone calling for the return of the monarchy or the restitution of the constitution of 1793 faced execution. A new law allowed the police to control the press. The police arrested and deported forty-two royalist journalists and editors.

And, once again, the French stirred anger outside their borders. While sailing to Egypt, Bonaparte had stopped to capture the island of Malta (off the coast of southern Italy). The czar of Russia, Paul I, considered himself to be Malta's protector. Insulted by Bonaparte's actions, he led Russia into the second coalition against France. Russian forces invaded French-occupied Italy. Here the people rose up against the French. The combination of Russian soldiers and Italian guerrillas drove the French from all the territory Bonaparte had conquered during his Italian campaign. Other allied armies attacked French forces along the Rhine River and in Holland. Suddenly, France was again isolated and surrounded by enemies, just as had been the case back in 1793.

> **FAST FACT**
>
> A COUP BY THE DIRECTORY IN SEPTEMBER 1797 LED TO THE ANNULMENT OF ELECTION RESULTS IN MORE THAN HALF THE COUNTRY AND REPLACEMENT OF MORE THAN 177 JACOBIN AND ROYALIST DEPUTIES.

The Directory had hoped to bring political stability to France in the aftermath of the chaos that followed the king's demise. It had hoped to create a moderate, liberal parliamentary system. In the end, it failed to do either. The Directory did have some accomplishments. It brought finances under control, reformed the tax system, and introduced advances in secondary education. But these reforms mostly benefited the bourgeoisie, while life for the poor only grew worse. The Directory had little support among the people. And when it finally collapsed, few in France were sorry to see it end.

CHAPTER 7

Order in the Aftermath of Revolution

A S SUPPORT FOR THE DIRECTORY fell, the desire for stability in France grew. The Revolution and the chaos that followed in its aftermath had drained the French spirit. The Revolution had not brought about the promised changes for most of France's population. And those who had tried to steer a new course had also failed. By the 1790s, the people were tired. They were tired of corrupt leaders. They were tired of violence. They were tired of instability. The French people were ready for a change. They were ready for a new leader who would not just make promises. They were ready for a leader who would deliver on those promises. They wanted stability. And they would get it, in the form of a new absolute ruler—Napoléon Bonaparte.

A CRITICAL JUNCTURE

During 1798 and the first half of 1799, the government of the Directory grew ever more unpopular. The corruption of the directors was apparent to most people. The diplomat Charles Talleyrand-Périgord returned to Paris and observed that "the words of Republic, Liberty, Equality, Fraternity, were everywhere inscribed on all the walls, but the ideas and feelings they expressed were nowhere to be met with." In June 1799, one politician attacked the Directory with these words: "You have destroyed civic virtue, gagged liberty, persecuted the republicans, suppressed the newspapers and suffocated the truth."

These charges were accurate. During the Revolution, many newspapers, journals, and pamphlets appeared. They held lively discussions of politics, and readership soared. This was unheard of in France, where press censorship was the norm. In the aftermath of the

> *"You have destroyed civic virtue, gagged liberty, persecuted the republicans, suppressed the newspapers and suffocated the truth."*
>
> —H. G. Bertrand, member of the council of 500, June 1799

Revolution, new ways of thinking and speaking had opened up, and these could all be found in the French press. So when the Directory clamped down on the press, the public was not pleased. Support for the Directory fell even further.

Unrest spread across France. Antigovernment rebels rose again in Brittany. The threat of royalist insurrection grew too. The ongoing

THE FRENCH DIPLOMAT CHARLES DE TALLEYRAND-PÉRIGORD
OBSERVED THAT LIBERTY, EQUALITY, AND FRATERNITY WERE NOWHERE
TO BE SEEN IN THE STREETS OF PARIS. THIS NINETEENTH-CENTURY
OIL PAINTING IS BY ARY SCHEFFER.

political chaos resulted in an overwhelming desire for change and stability. One dedicated royalist who had survived the Terror spoke for most Frenchmen when he explained that he and his friends were prepared to support any government that possessed "a sincere desire to restore order in France."

The lack of confidence in civilian rule and the desire for stability led to a search for military men to serve on the five-man Directory. When General François Lefebvre received votes to fill a place on the

Directory, his wife observed, "They must be in a bad way when they want to make a dolt like you a King!"

Prominent civilians and soldiers jointly denounced the Directory. Legislators understood that reform without constitutional change was impossible. Few had any scruples about employing force to accomplish it.

FAST FACT

BETWEEN ABOUT 1789 AND 1799, FRANCE HAD FOUR DIFFERENT CONSTITUTIONS.

However, power was divided among many factions. On the left stood the Jacobins, on the right the royalists. In the middle were ardent republicans who sincerely believed that in spite of the hysteria and bloodshed of the Revolution, it had promoted important ideals worth defending. To succeed, each faction needed a leader willing to risk all to execute a coup, a man who possessed a reputation to attract sufficient followers. At this juncture, thirty-year-old Napoléon Bonaparte returned to France.

THE COUP OF BRUMAIRE

One of the directors, Emmanuel-Joseph Sieyès, had been looking for a military man to help him mount a coup that would appear to be legal. Napoléon Bonaparte seemed to fill the bill. Together they hatched a plot to overthrow the government. The plot involved three phases. On the first day, the *Anciens* (Council of the Elders) would announce the discovery of a Jacobin conspiracy. For safety, members of the government would be asked to move to a new location. Second, Bonaparte's soldiers would provide security for this move and thus be in a position to act if the plotters required such action. During the third phase, the legislature would revise the constitution.

Despite the unexpected threat of violent resistance by members of the government, the Coup of Brumaire (November 18–19, 1799, named after the date in the revolutionary calendar) succeeded. The legislature appointed three officials to serve as a provisional (temporary) government, including Sieyès and Bonaparte. Bonaparte's position as provisional consul proved temporary. His coconspirators had thought that they could control Bonaparte. They quickly perceived their error. The night after the coup, Sieyès observed, "We have a master who knows how to do everything, who can do everything, and who wishes to do everything."

THE COUP OF BRUMAIRE IN NOVEMBER 1799 ENABLED BONAPARTE, CENTER, TO BECOME FIRST CONSUL OF FRANCE. THIS NINETEENTH-CENTURY OIL PAINTING IS BY FRANÇOIS BOUCHOT.

"To the Army"

THROUGHOUT HIS CAREER, Napoléon displayed an exceptional ability to inspire soldiers. In March 1796, for the first time in his career, the young general Napoléon Bonaparte took command of an entire army. He found this force camped in the Italian mountains where it was dispirited and near mutiny. He issued the following proclamation to the Army of Italy:

> Soldiers! You are hungry and naked; the government owes you much but can give you nothing. The patience and courage which you have displayed among these rocks are admirable; but they bring you no glory—not a glimmer falls upon you. I will lead you into the most fertile plains on earth. Rich provinces, opulent towns, all shall be at your disposal; there you will find honour, glory, and riches. Soldiers of Italy! Will you be lacking in courage or endurance?

Napoléon's appeal to personal glory, his personal relationships with his soldiers, and his own willingness to face the dangers of battle led his soldiers to feel great loyalty for their leader.

Indeed, soon after the coup, Bonaparte emerged as first consul, the leader of the government. On December 25, 1799, he and his fellow consuls presented France with a new constitution. The fact that this was France's fourth new constitution in the past ten years underscored how much change had come in the aftermath of the Revolution.

Bonaparte had a decisive voice in writing the constitution. It gave the first consul nearly limitless power. Bonaparte knew that the people wanted a return to more stable times. So, in a written declaration, he announced that the violence and chaos of the revolutionary period had ended: "Citizens, the Revolution is confined to the principles which commenced it: it is finished." The Coup of Brumaire and the rise of Napoléon Bonaparte mark an endpoint for the French Revolution. Years of dictatorial rule would follow in its aftermath.

EMPEROR NAPOLÉON

As first consul, Bonaparte led a French army over the Alps into Italy. Here he defeated the Austrians at the decisive Battle of Marengo on June 14, 1800. Later victories on other fronts led to the second coalition's collapse and the Peace of Amiens on March 27, 1802. After more than a decade of conflict, France was at peace.

The Peace of Amiens ended the revolutionary wars. France had won a complete victory. Bonaparte's rise to power ended Louis XVIII's hopes that he could return to rule France. Louis XVIII and his supporters concluded that they had to do something extraordinary to overthrow Bonaparte. They mounted an assassination attempt that narrowly failed. After that failure, Louis XVIII's chance to restore his dynasty's rule depended on the military defeat of France by European nations. Indeed, a new war between France and a host of enemies resumed after barely a year of peace.

In the Revolution's aftermath, even while engaged in war, First Consul Napoléon Bonaparte set about reforming France. One of the controversial actions of the revolutionary government had been the suppression of the Catholic Church. Bonaparte considered it a mistake. He wanted to rally French Catholics to support his government. So he took actions to heal the divide between France and the church. The result was an agreement

> **FAST FACT**
>
> THE CONCORDAT, SIGNED ON JULY 15, 1801, REESTABLISHED THE CATHOLIC CHURCH IN FRANCE.

with the pope. Signed on July 15, 1801, the agreement—called the Concordat—reestablished the Catholic Church in France and opened the way for the clergy to return.

The French government made other important changes under Napoléon. It granted amnesty (legal pardon) to the émigrés

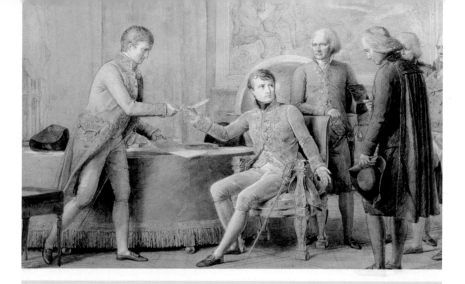

On July 15, 1801, Napoléon signed the Concordat, which reestablished the Catholic Church in France.

and returned their property. It created state-sponsored schools. It brought about many constructive financial reforms, including the creation of the Bank of France and a simpler tax system.

The legislature prepared a new legal code to regulate society. Known as the Civil Code (or Code Napoléon), it came into effect in March 1804. The Civil Code is considered the most solid and lasting accomplishment of Napoléon's rule. The code created a uniform legal system, applicable to all individuals in France. Before the code, laws varied from province to province. Some of these laws dated back before the Revolution. Some grew out of the Revolution. Napoléon did not invent the code, but he knew the importance of having a uniform system of civil laws. And his efforts in this area influenced modern civil law around the world. Many aspects of the Civil Code remain French law today.

In the aftermath of the Revolution, the French people had wanted stability, efficiency, and prosperity. Napoléon Bonaparte provided it. But it came at a cost: Bonaparte transformed the consular republic into a monarchy. On December 2, 1804, Paris witnessed the coronation of Emperor Napoléon I. In a stunning display of personal power, Napoléon took the imperial crown from the pope and placed it on his own head (rather than following the longstanding tradition of the pope crowning the emperor). He then crowned his wife Josephine as empress. These acts were deliberate symbols to emphasize that Napoléon yielded to no power other than his own. During his coronation oath, he swore to govern the nation "only in accordance

Coalitions Against France

The nations of Europe formed no fewer than seven alliances against France—called coalitions—between 1792 and 1815. The first coalition began in 1792 with Austria and Prussia uniting against revolutionary France. Great Britain and Spain joined the following year. Russia, Holland, Naples, and Tuscany also took part. The coalition began falling apart in 1795 and 1796 as the members made separate peace agreements with France. Austria fought on alone until 1797.

By 1799 the second coalition formed, first between Great Britain and Austria and later joined by Russia. It ended in 1802. Napoléon's wars of empire forced the formation of the third coalition by 1805. Great Britain, Austria, Russia, and Sweden allied themselves against Napoléon, but the coalition did not last the year. In 1806, Prussia, Russia, and Great Britain formed the fourth coalition. This too ended in defeat within a year. The fifth coalition, formed in 1809, consisted of Austria and Great Britain. Austria quickly went down in defeat, leaving the British to fight on alone in Portugal and Spain.

When Napoléon invaded Russia in 1812, Russia and Great Britain formed the sixth coalition, to be joined later by Spain, Portugal, Prussia, Austria, and Sweden. This proved to be the coalition that drove Napoléon from his throne in 1814. When Napoléon returned from exile to reclaim control of France, the same allies formed the seventh coalition. Their combined strength administered an overwhelming defeat in 1815.

with the interests, the happiness, and the glory of the French people."
Events would show that he alone interpreted what this oath meant.
In this way, he was an absolute monarch.

The contemporary nineteenth-century French author, François
Chateaubriand, was a fierce critic of Napoléon. He wrote, "Under the
Empire [of Napoleonic rule], we [the French people] disappeared;
there was no longer any mention of us, and everything belonged to
Bonaparte: 'I have ordered, I have conquered, I have spoken; my
eagles [an emblem carried by French soldiers], my crown, my blood,
my family, my subjects.'" Indeed, the French Revolution began as
a revolt against privilege as represented by King Louis XVI. In its
aftermath, France saw the installation of a new ruler, another absolute monarch. This ruler shared the identical attitude of past French
kings—that he alone could judge what was best for his people.

Fifteen more years of war, which historians label the Napoleonic
Wars, followed the Revolution. Napoléon was one of history's rare military geniuses. His combination of genius and hard work built Europe's
most powerful war machine. Napoléon used his armies to conquer
France's neighbors and create the Napoleonic Empire. Over the period
from 1805 to 1808, French armies defeated the armies of Austria, Russia, Prussia, and Spain. It seemed like nothing could stop Napoléon
from establishing and maintaining control of all of Europe.

Great Britain was the one constant enemy that persisted against
Napoléon. Protected by its royal navy, Great Britain continued to
support Napoléon's enemies on the continent of Europe. At the
same time, it provided shelter and support to the French royalists
who opposed Napoléon.

With only a few interruptions, between 1808 and 1815, Great
Britain and a changing cast of European nations waged war to overthrow Napoléon. Finally, on June 18, 1815, the British and Prussian
armies defeated Napoléon for a final time at the Battle of Waterloo

THE AFTERMATH OF THE FRENCH REVOLUTION

What Napoléon Believed

Napoléon was a man of immense talents who regularly worked harder than anyone else. Here are some of his thoughts:

On Liberty and Equality: "Liberty is a need felt by a small class of people whom nature has endowed with nobler minds than the mass of men. Consequently, it may be repressed with impunity [without punishment]. Equality, on the other hand, pleases the masses."

On Democracy: "Democracy, if it is reasonable, limits itself to giving everyone an equal opportunity to compete and to obtain."

On Mastering Fortune: "What I am, I owe to strength of will, character, application, and daring."

in Belgium. The victors sent Napoléon into exile on the bleak South Atlantic Ocean island of St. Helena.

THE RETURN OF THE KINGS

Then, what had seemed impossible on January 21, 1793, the day Louis XVI faced the guillotine, came to pass. Another king, Louis XVIII, returned for good in 1815 and ruled until his death in 1824. He tried to steer a moderate course. Chateaubriand observed, "I witnessed the third transformation of society within my lifetime: I had seen the old monarchy [Louis XVI] turn into the constitutional monarchy, and the latter into the Republic; I had seen the Republic change into military despotism [the consulate and empire of Napoléon Bonaparte]; and now I was seeing military despotism turning back into a free monarchy, the new ideas and the new generations returning to the old principles and the old men."

WHEN LOUIS XVIII CAME TO THE THRONE IN 1815, HE TRIED TO STEER FRANCE ON A MODERATE COURSE UNTIL HIS DEATH IN 1824. THIS NINETEENTH-CENTURY OIL PAINTING IS BY FRANÇOIS GERARD.

Charles X, brother of Louis XVIII, succeeded him to the throne and tried to turn back the clock to the prerevolutionary days of absolute monarchy. By 1830 Charles X appeared ready to cast away the last remnants of the Revolution. He dissolved the elected Chamber of Deputies and sharply curtailed freedom of the press. Paris responded with three days of public revolt that drove the king from power. His cousin, Louis-Philippe, showed that he supported the Revolution of 1789 by appearing before the mob alongside the elderly Marquis de Lafayette. Lafayette wrapped himself in the tricolor flag, the old symbol of the unity of the Paris rebels, whose colors were red and blue with the white of the monarchy. Lafayette embraced Louis-Philippe and the mob roared its approval. So, Louis-Philippe became king in 1830.

In another legacy of the revolution of 1789, Louis-Philippe was called the "Citizen-King." Unlike earlier monarchs, Louis-Philippe dressed and acted more like the middle-class bourgeoisie, which made him a popular ruler among French citizens. Yet after eighteen mostly stable years of monarchic rule, popular dissatisfaction with

The Changing Governments of France

From the start of the French Revolution in 1789 to the final defeat of Napoléon in 1815, the government of France changed seven times.

1. **Estates General:** The legislative arm of the French government under the monarchy, which lasted until May 1789.

2. **National Assembly:** Revolutionary elements in the Estates General organized under this name in June 1789.

3. **National Constituent Assembly:** The official name given to the government that replaced the Estates General in July 1789; this body created the Constitution of 1791. Extremists battled for control of the assembly and rendered it less than effective.

4. **Legislative Assembly:** Authorized by the Constitution of 1791, its elected representatives met from October 1791 to September 1792.

5. **National Convention:** Elected in September 1792, marking the beginning of the Republic, its changing cast of 745 deputies ruled France during the Terror. The convention created a new constitution in October 1795.

6. **Directory:** The Council of 500, ruled by five directors, replaced the National Convention in November 1795.

7. **Consulate:** In the coup engineered by Napoléon in November 1799, three consuls became the rulers of France. The following month the consulate presented a new constitution, under which Napoléon exercised the real power as first consul.

The French republic became an empire with the coronation of Emperor Napoléon I in 1804. He met his final defeat at the Battle of Waterloo in 1815, and the monarchy returned in the person of Louis XVIII, brother of the executed Louis XVI, in 1815.

the monarchy and its abuses of power led to increasing unrest. Again popular defiance drove the French king from power during the revolution of 1848. Louis-Napoléon Bonaparte, nephew of Napoléon I, became president of France. On December 2, 1852, the anniversary of Napoléon I's coronation, Louis-Napoléon was proclaimed Emperor Napoléon III of France.

In a little more than twenty years, France appeared to have come full circle. Revolution had swept away the monarchy, but it had failed to make France a democracy. In the aftermath of revolution, the monarchy was replaced first by a constitutional monarchy, then by a constitutional republic. What came next was almost complete anarchy (no government). This was replaced by an oligarchy, in which a small group runs the government. Then came military dictatorship, followed by yet another monarchy.

Yet much had changed in France during this time. Revolutionary leaders had hoped for a more enlightened society. Though greatly flawed, their effort succeeded in many ways. They reorganized the French educational system. One of their most lasting achievements was a system of free, universal schools for all children—rich or poor. The Revolution also changed many of the institutions and routines of private life. Almost overnight, for example, France's divorce laws became the most liberal in the world.

The Revolution and the era of Napoléon had given France the tools for developing a modern, more enlightened society. France had done away with feudalism and had created national legal codes, uniform weights and measures, equality before the law, and a national bank. Although French citizens did not enjoy political and civil liberties under Napoléon, his armies carried the reforms and ideals of the Revolution with them to all corners of Napoléon's vast empire. In this way, the French Revolution reached far beyond France's borders.

CHAPTER 8

Impact on Neighboring Nations

I N THE TIME LEADING UP TO the French Revolution, European powers dealt with France as they had always done. Political leaders saw France as a powerful enemy, a rival, or sometimes an ally. The revolution in France caught them by surprise.

For many people, news of the French Revolution was romantic and thrilling. Until this point in Western history, revolutionary change had taken place only in America. But in European minds, the American Revolution had been a unique situation since it took place in a distant part of the world. In contrast, the French Revolution had occurred in Europe. This inspired people to think that major reforms elsewhere in Europe were possible.

For example, when the influential British politician Charles James Fox heard about the storming of the Bastille, he wrote: "How much the greatest event it is that ever happened in the world! and how much the best!" Likewise, a Russian diplomat said, "The cry of freedom rings in my ears and the best day of my life will be that when I see a Russia regenerated by such a Revolution." Belgian rebels chose a rallying cry of "Here as in Paris!"

> *"The cry of freedom rings in my ears."*
>
> —a Russian diplomat, 1789

As a result of the French Revolution, all around Europe, people interested in politics joined clubs, formed associations, and attended conventions. They discussed the role of the citizen and argued about what was meant by the rights of man. They considered new constitutions and issued manifestos (written demands) calling for change.

Thereafter, people watched events in France with a mixture of admiration, horror, and fear. The countries opposed to France expressed concern for the French royal family, the church, and the émigrés. But what the leaders of such nations as Great Britain, Prussia, Austria, and Russia were really worried about was that the "revolutionary virus," as they called it, might spread to their own countries and infect their own people. Their response was deeply conservative. Their leaders emphasized respect for tradition and the importance of maintaining the existing structure of society.

THE POLITICAL IMPACT OF THE REVOLUTION ON GREAT BRITAIN

The French Revolution's chaos and violence shocked most Britons. The execution of King Louis XVI roused the British to oppose France. Newspapers carried headlines condemning the king's murderers. The theaters closed for three days. People wore mourning clothes. Ten days after the execution, France declared war on Great Britain. Many Britons saw this as an opportunity to seek revenge. King George III of Great Britain said he expected his nation to rally against France with such spirit "that I trust will curb the insolence of those despots [the French rebel leaders] and be a means of restoring some degree of order to that unprincipled country, whose aim at present is to destroy the foundations of every civilised state."

In spite of the execution of King Louis XVI and the subsequent Terror, the ideals of the Revolution continued to appeal to some British political leaders. They formed a party known as the Radicals, who opposed the ruling British political party. Others such as Edmund Burke, a conservative member of the British House of Commons, expressed alarm at events in France. Though Burke had supported the American colonies in their war for independence and advocated reforms in England, he condemned the French Revolution and the violence that grew from it.

In 1790, Burke published *Reflections on the Revolution in France.* In it he argued that the French Revolution was an assault on tradition. Burke wrote that criticism of an existing form of government only invited anarchy, and that this was a formula for disaster that must be avoided in Britain. *Reflections on the Revolution in France* was the classic conservative response to the challenges posed by the French Revolution.

Burke's writings prompted a response from those who still admired the revolution. None responded more eloquently than the American revolutionary Thomas Paine. In February 1791, Paine published *The Rights of Man.* He urged Britons to follow the French example. So began a decade-long debate pitting Burke and the conservatives against Paine and the reformers.

The radicals continued to work to reform British society in general and Parliament in particular. In 1794, the British government brought many radical leaders to trial on the charge of treason. But in contrast to the failure of the French legal system to protect the people against tyranny, the British system of justice triumphed. It acquitted the radical leaders. This proved a great blow against the British government.

In the autumn of 1794, a mob threatened George III while he was on his way to Parliament in London. This was exactly the kind of behavior that worried conservatives in the British government. The government thought that lawless mob behavior stemmed from the influence of French propaganda. To limit this possibility, the British government suspended the right of habeas corpus for seven years. This

IN THIS NINETEENTH-CENTURY OIL PAINTING, BRITISH LAWMAKER EDMUND BURKE, FAR RIGHT, IS SHOWN WITH MEMBERS OF HIS LITERARY CLUB. BURKE WROTE A CONSERVATIVE RESPONSE TO THE CHALLENGES OF THE FRENCH REVOLUTION.

THIS ENGLISH HAND-COLORED POLITICAL CARTOON BY HANNAH HUMPHREY
FROM 1795 DEPICTS THE BRITISH MOB THREATENING KING GEORGE III
IN HIS CARRIAGE. ACTS LIKE THIS CAUSED THE BRITISH GOVERNMENT TO
SUSPEND HABEAS CORPUS IN BRITAIN FOR SEVEN YEARS.

right protects people from unlawful arrest and detention. By suspending this right, the government, without producing evidence, could arrest and detain people suspected of opposing the government.

REBELS EVERYWHERE?

The ability of the French people to overthrow their king excited the imagination of many people throughout Europe. They too wanted significant social and political change. Those who lived in nearby

A FRENCH VICTORY OVER THE AUSTRIANS AT THE BATTLE OF
JEMAPPES IN 1792 ENABLED FRANCE TO ANNEX BELGIUM IN 1793.
THIS ANONYMOUS PAINTING IS FROM 1793.

countries expected that France's revolutionary government would happily support them. One such country was Belgium.

In 1789, Belgium was part of the Hapsburg Empire (modern Austria formed the core of this empire). Inspired by the French Revolution, Belgian patriots tried to revolt against Austrian control. Their effort failed.

Three years later, in 1792, a French army defeated the Austrians at the Battle of Jemappes in Belgium. The victory allowed the French to occupy most of Belgium. Belgian patriots resurfaced and greeted the French as liberators. At first, the French supported the idea of an independent Belgian republic. However, France needed Belgian resources to support its own wars. Consequently, France annexed (took over) Belgium in 1793. Thereafter, the Belgian people had the same rights as French citizens. They also had the same obligations— most importantly to use French paper money and to contribute men and supplies for the French wars.

Like Belgium, Holland was part of the Hapsburg Empire. Belgium's fate distressed Dutch patriots. They neither wanted to be occupied by the French nor annexed into the French Republic. In 1794, French armies won important victories in northwestern Europe. These victories encouraged Dutch revolutionaries to proclaim a new independent state called the Batavian Republic. For three years, the French occupied the Batavian Republic but allowed the Dutch the freedom to create their own government. However, the Dutch proved unable to reach a political agreement about the form of their government. Dutch royalists wanted a return to the traditional ways. Dutch democrats wanted French-style changes.

Changes in the Map of Europe

THE FRENCH REVOLUTION triggered a series of European wars. By the time they were over, the map of Europe had been redrawn. Many of these changes became permanent. The Austrian emperor had been the head of Europe's oldest political body, the Holy Roman Empire. It had lasted for some one thousand years. But the combination of the wars of the Revolution and the Napoleonic Wars put an end to the Holy Roman Empire. The Austrian emperor lost his title and Austria lost significant territory including control of Belgium and the Netherlands. This paved the way for the formation of two independent nations, the Dutch republic and Belgium.

Moving east and south on the map, Luxembourg also became an independent duchy. Along the Rhine River, numerous small principalities disappeared, eventually absorbed by Prussia. The city-republic of Geneva, Switzerland, likewise disappeared, absorbed by the Swiss republic. Other great city-states in northern Italy, including the once-powerful Venetian republic, were swept away by French military power. The rearranging of Italian territory continued into the middle of the nineteenth century until a united Italy emerged.

In 1797 the French intervened. France wanted above all else an organized Dutch government that would help France in its war against Great Britain. The result was that Holland served as a French ally during most of the Revolutionary Wars and the ensuing Napoleonic Wars. However, certain enduring changes did occur—an outgrowth of France's experience with revolution. Because of the French influence, the Dutch achieved equality of civil rights, a reduction in religious controls, and fiscal, legal, and administrative reforms.

GERMANY BYPASSED

One region where the French Revolution had small influence was a close neighbor, the German principalities east of the Rhine River. In 1789, the modern state of Germany did not exist. Instead about three hundred small states called principalities were ruled by nobles or religious leaders. In addition, about fifty free cities were ruled by hereditary leaders. Only in the eastern part of Germany was there a large, unified German state. This was Prussia, with its capital in Berlin. Both in the small German states and in Prussia, people had a great respect for authority. In most of the small German states, a professional class of civil servants managed governmental affairs. They did not worry about public opinion and found it easy to ignore the upheaval in nearby France. In Prussia the middle class was generally sympathetic to the French Revolution but saw no need for similar changes in Prussia. A Prussian minister explained this attitude to a French visitor in 1799: "The salutary [beneficial] revolution which you made from below [among the masses] will take place gradually here in Prussia." He added that the Prussian king was already working to limit the privileges of the nobility.

During the Napoleonic Wars, France organized the smaller German states into a confederation that supported the French war effort. This period witnessed many German legislative reforms based on the French model of the Civil Code.

The reforms occurred without violence. Rather, existing governments enacted the reforms. Even while challenges to authority were occurring nearby, limited reforms came to Germany without disrespect to or violence against authority.

The aftermath of the French Revolution had its greatest impact in Germany in the development of German political thinking. Three great German philosophers—Immanuel Kant, Johann Fichte, and Georg Hegel—lived during the French Revolution and its aftermath and were inspired by it in developing their philosophical theories.

The French Revolution also led indirectly to the rise of German nationalism. The French armies under Napoléon crushed Prussia in 1806. The defeat shocked Prussian military and political leaders. Thoughtful Prussian leaders worked to understand what had happened. One of them, a military officer named Augustus von Gneisenau, concluded, "One cause above all has raised France to the pinnacle of greatness. The Revolution awakened all her powers and gave each individual a suitable field for his activity."

Gneisenau and his followers set about making military reforms based on the French model. To accomplish their goal, they convinced the Prussian king to appeal to the German sense of nationalism just as revolutionary leaders in France had appealed to the French sense of patriotism. The appeal worked brilliantly. In 1813

INSPIRED BY THE FRENCH MODEL, PRUSSIA'S AUGUSTUS VON
GNEISENAU, ON HORSEBACK, CENTER, AND HIS FOLLOWERS INSTITUTED
MILITARY REFORMS TO THE PRUSSIAN ARMY. THIS ANONYMOUS OIL
PAINTING IS FROM 1815.

tens of thousands of young Germans mobilized to fight what Prussian historians called "The War of Liberation" against France. In 1815, the Prussian army played a decisive role helping to defeat Napoléon during the Waterloo Campaign.

Later, during the 1860s, German nationalism motivated the drive toward German unification. After Prussia merged with all of the smaller German states, Germany became a world power. From at least the time of the Franco-Prussian War (1870) until World War II (1939–1945), German affairs dominated Europe. A strong, nationalistic Germany sought to impose itself on the rest of Europe.

Switzerland

In the eighteenth century, Switzerland was a loose association of thirteen German-speaking regions called cantons. The Italian- and French-speaking regions, and some German regions, were independent and self-governing. But everywhere in Switzerland, an entrenched aristocracy ruled. Swiss democrats wanted change. In 1790, Swiss residents in Paris formed political clubs to discuss reform and revolution. They exchanged ideas with radicals living in Switzerland. Pro-revolutionary uprisings soon followed in some parts of Switzerland. Rebels in Vaud, for example, rallied with a French-style call of "Liberty and Country."

The French revolutionary government was too busy with problems of its own to help the Swiss rebels. The result was that the Swiss aristocracy made some concessions to the rebels but retained power. Yet when France's self-interest was at stake, France did intervene in Swiss affairs because of the issue of French émigrés, many of whom had taken refuge in Switzerland. Initially, the French government demanded the expulsion of the émigrés. At the same time, French agents spread revolutionary propaganda in Switzerland. Their goal was to create unrest so France would have a good excuse to intervene in Switzerland with military force.

> ## Fast Fact
> The French Revolution gave birth to French nationalism, which in turn influenced the rise of nationalism in other countries.

In 1797 French forces occupied Geneva, Switzerland. This prompted other Swiss cantons to make quick, democratic reforms in the hope that they would not be occupied next. However, French leaders also had military goals in Switzerland. They wanted control of the strategic mountain passes connecting Switzerland with Italy. So, French forces seized more Swiss territory. On March 28, 1798, the French proclaimed that they had taken over governmental authority in Switzerland. The French created a new Swiss entity called the Helvetic Republic.

At first, the French introduced significant reforms. Henceforth all citizens were equal before the law. The French abolished class distinctions and many of the privileges enjoyed by the aristocracy. But as time passed, the reality of French interest in Switzerland became clear. The French government was more interested in the role Switzerland could play in its wars against Austria and the other coalition powers than in allowing Switzerland to become a true republic.

This discovery was disillusioning for Swiss republicans and other Europeans, who came to realize that the new French leaders were not so different from the old. Like monarchs before them, the revolutionary leaders placed the security of France ahead of the political ideals of liberty and equality.

ITALY

In 1796 a French army commanded by Napoléon Bonaparte had invaded northern Italy. At this time, Italy was not a unified state but a collection of numerous independent duchies, city-states, and territory controlled by the Catholic Church. The Hapsburg Empire dominated most of northern Italy.

Napoléon Bonaparte fought a brilliant campaign that drove the Austrians eastward and out of Italy. Behind the French armies came French administrators who wanted to exploit the conquered territory in order to support the war. The French enlisted sympathetic Italians to govern the province of Lombardy. Just as had occurred in Belgium and Holland, the Italians soon set to work to create an Italian republic.

Italian leaders sponsored an essay contest on the subject "Which form of free government is best suited to Italy?" They organized a pro-French fighting force and gave it a flag with red, white, and green stripes. This flag later became the flag of the modern Italian state. In 1797 Napoléon Bonaparte authorized the creation of the Cisalpine Republic. It was a brand-new territorial creation made from parts of six other Italian states and cities. Revolutionaries, reformers, and republicans from all over Italy came to the new republic's capital at Milan. They formed clubs, published revolutionary literature, and talked of overthrowing the pope and the king of Naples.

The Cisalpine Republic adopted the programs of the French Revolution. It abolished the nobility, did away with the guilds (early exclusive trade groups), removed education from church control, and

THE COUNCIL OF THE CISALPINE REPUBLIC, BELOW, PROCLAIMS NAPOLÉON BONAPARTE, RIGHT, SEATED, THEIR PRESIDENT ON JANUARY 26, 1802, AS SHOWN IN THIS OIL PAINTING FROM 1802 BY NICOLAS ANDRÉ MONSIAU.

much else. In many ways, the Cisalpine Republic marks the birth of modern Italy.

By looking over the span of European history, a path of cause and effect can be traced. The French Revolution had given birth to French nationalism. In turn, the aggressive pressure of French nationalism on other European nations had caused the birth of German nationalism. Consider the words of a French official during the Revolution: "We shall turn France into a cemetery rather than fail in her regeneration." Compare these words to a song sung by German Nazi soldiers in the 1930s: "What does it matter if we destroy the world? When it is ours, we'll build it up again."

In the centuries since the French Revolution, individuals and nations around the world have looked back on these events as a model. The French Revolution is seen as a model of oppressed people rising up, fighting for sweeping political and social change, and claiming the universal rights of liberty and equality. In this sense, the French Revolution not only influenced the course of events for the French people but for people around the world.

CHAPTER 9

Far-Reaching Influence of the Revolution

THE FRENCH REVOLUTION DIRECTLY affected France's closest neighbors. However, its influence did not stop there. News of the revolution spread around the world. The rapid political and social changes that had taken place in France were unlike anything in living memory. The French Revolution excited hope among the downtrodden for more rights and a better life while it stunned and frightened the ruling classes. Every country responded to the Revolution in its own way.

IRELAND

With the backing of England, a small Protestant minority who belonged to the Episcopalian Church dominated Ireland. The Roman Catholic majority was banned from public positions of power. The French Revolution changed these relationships. In response to the outbreak of war with revolutionary France, the British government made reforms in 1793 designed to ensure Irish Catholic loyalty. Catholics received the right to vote and participate in public affairs. These reforms failed to satisfy some Irish political leaders.

British authorities feared the effect of French revolutionary propaganda on the Irish. Their fears were realized when the outbreak of the French Revolution prompted some Irish intellectuals to overcome their religious differences and unite against British rule. One of their leaders was the radical young Irish lawyer Wolfe Tone. Tone and his fellow radicals founded societies of United Irishmen, which became clubs seeking social and political change.

WOLFE TONE, SEATED, CENTER, AND HIS SOCIETIES OF UNITED IRISHMEN SOUGHT SUPPORT FROM REVOLUTIONARY FRANCE AGAINST BRITISH RULE IN IRELAND. THIS IRISH SCHOOL LITHOGRAPH IS FROM THE NINETEENTH CENTURY.

THE AFTERMATH OF THE FRENCH REVOLUTION

When British authorities drove these clubs underground, Irish radicals sought military support from revolutionary France. France sent several military expeditions to Ireland, but they failed. Nonetheless, in 1798 the United Irishmen launched a pro-French revolt. Although it too failed, it brought the relationship between Ireland and Great Britain to the forefront of British politics. The result was the merging of the kingdoms of Great Britain and Ireland into the United Kingdom. This measure came into effect in 1801. In this way, the French Revolution decisively changed Irish history.

POLAND

Ireland was not the only land to feel the effects of the French Revolution. The ripples of the French Revolution made a particular impact in Poland. In 1791 Polish reformers produced a new constitution. Just as in Paris, political clubs formed to debate the issues of the day. A free press developed. For a brief time, Poles enjoyed freedom of speech.

The Polish constitution of 1791 was far more conservative than the new French constitution. But, it granted enough new rights to Polish citizens to be considered revolutionary by the nations on Poland's borders. These nations—Russia, Prussia, and Austria—worried that the French revolutionary virus had spread to Poland. They feared it might spread farther into their own lands, so they decided to eliminate the threat.

In the past, these nations worried about France as a traditional Polish ally. However, revolutionary France appeared weak. So, Russia invaded Poland. A brief war ensued after which Russia, Prussia, and Austria carved up Poland into what became known as the Second Polish Partition. They left a small area under the control of Poles.

This area revolted again in 1793. The rebels changed much, including the Polish language. In the past, the Polish word for "citizen" meant nobles only. Henceforth, it meant everyone. The old Polish word for "nation" also meant only the nobility. The new word meant the entire Polish people.

One rebel leader, Thaddeus Kosciuszko, understood that the Polish people had to be given an interest to inspire their fight. Kosciuszko said, "Victory will go to those who fight in their own cause." However, in contrast to the French Revolution, Polish revolutionary leaders avoided radical reforms. Instead the aristocracy and the reformers compromised.

The Polish rebel leaders issued their own version of the levée en masse (military draft). They encouraged the Polish peasants to join the army. However, they also said that after the war, the peasants would continue to labor according to the old, traditional system, which offered few benefits to the peasants. For this reason, the approach failed to inspire the peasants.

Again Poland's neighbors judged the revolt a serious threat to their own rule. They blamed the revolt on the French. The Russian empress claimed that "the wanton Warsaw horde" (referring to that Polish city's masses) had been created by "French tyrants." The king of Prussia said that the Polish revolt showed "the diabolical [evil] activity deployed by the [French] Jacobins to light the fire of sedition [treason] in every corner of Europe."

The Russian and Prussian armies squashed the Polish revolt in 1794. They divided the conquered land in the Third Partition. An independent Poland disappeared from the map of Europe.

POLISH PATRIOT THADDEUS KOSCIUSZKO LED A REVOLT IN 1793 AGAINST THE AUSTRIAN AND RUSSIAN PARTITIONING OF POLAND.

RUSSIA

Before the French Revolution, class distinctions divided Russia more than in any other European country. The nobility enjoyed numerous rights and possessed most of the wealth. They bought and sold peasants, called serfs, and treated them as slaves. At the same time, they lived in fear of serf revolts, which broke out from time to time. The privileged classes therefore resisted the radical revolutionary notions of "liberté" and "égalité."

The Russian empress Catherine II, known as Catherine the Great, particularly hated the French Revolution. This was a major reason Russia worked so hard to crush Poland. Catherine II and the czars (heads of state) who followed her worried that if the seed of revolution grew in Poland, it might spread to Russia. As Catherine II said, she "would fight Jacobinism and beat it in Poland."

Yet news of the French Revolution seeped into Russia. In response, Russian rulers cracked down on potential reformers. One instance involved a journalist named N. I. Novikov. Novikov edited a journal directed at non-noble readers. Novikov also managed a school for translators of foreign books and opened a public library in Moscow. The Russian authorities had always feared the free exchange of ideas, and the French Revolution reinforced their fear. They sentenced Novikov to fifteen years in prison. Likewise, Russian authorities sent into exile in Siberia another Russian journalist who published a favorable piece on American liberty.

All the same, news of the French Revolution continued to spread through Russia. In 1793 unknown authors circulated a pamphlet that supported the rights of man while challenging the rights of property and nobility. But such pamphlets failed to make a significant impact.

The Russian noble class remained firmly in charge of the government and the nation. From time to time, they issued patriotic calls to the serfs, summoning them to war against the French. The nobles cited French attacks against religion as proof that the French were a disreputable, godless society. The Russian government's appeals to patriotism and religion worked. Although serf rebellions continued to break out, overall the common Russian people supported the government against foreign invasions. Brave, patriotic serfs filled the ranks of the czar's armies. Russian soldiers fought hard against the armies of revolutionary France. They proved crucial in bringing about Napoléon's downfall.

RUSSIAN EMPRESS CATHERINE THE GREAT WAS A DETERMINED FOE OF THE FRENCH REVOLUTION. THIS OIL PAINTING IS FROM THE NINETEENTH CENTURY.

RUSSIAN REVOLUTIONARIES, INSPIRED BY SOME OF THE IDEALS OF THE FRENCH REVOLUTION, MARCH THROUGH THE STREETS OF PETROGRAD DURING THE RUSSIAN REVOLUTION OF 1917.

The Russian nobility managed to hold on to power until 1917. In 1917 came the Russian Revolution, which toppled hereditary czarist rule. Although the Russian Revolution arose from circumstances unique to Russia, many Russian revolutionaries cited the French Revolution as inspiration. A few months after revolutionaries seized control of the Russian government, they erected a statue of Robespierre in Moscow. The statue was symbolic of the link between the Russian revolutionaries and the French Jacobins.

THE HAPSBURG EMPIRE

The rulers of the Hapsburg Empire also felt the tremors of the French Revolution. From their capital in Vienna, Hapsburg officials gazed out at an empire united by weak bonds. The empire encompassed people of many different ethnic backgrounds including Germans,

Czechs, and Hungarians. The Austrian core was solid. But in 1775, a peasant rebellion had arisen among the Czechs in Bohemia. In 1790, a peasant rebellion swept Hungary.

The peasants knew that the Hapsburg emperor, Joseph II, had tried to improve their lives by ending serfdom. They knew that the nobility had defended its privileged position and blocked this effort. They heard the news of the French Revolution, with its demand of "liberté" and "égalité." It was an appealing call for the peasants. Then, they learned that their government had gone to war against revolutionary France. Some wondered if their own government was not the real enemy.

Hapsburg officials worked to tamp down any possibility of a French-style revolt. They circulated German translations of Burke's *Reflections on the French Revolution*. They spread word of French atrocities in order to alarm peasants and make them fearful of change.

More than anyplace else, Hungary resisted the Hapsburg government's propaganda efforts. Hungarians had a long history of opposing central rule from Vienna. Hungarian nationalists translated the "Marseillaise"

FAST FACT

AS LATE AS 1800, 90 PERCENT OF PEASANTS LIVING ON THE ESTATE OF THE AUSTRIAN EMPEROR'S BROTHER SUPPORTED THE FRENCH.

so the people could read its inspiring call for bloody rebellion. Some read newspapers brought from France to keep informed about the French Revolution. Some formed secret groups and plotted revolt.

But the Hapsburg secret police were watching closely. They arrested the plotters and executed twenty of them. Still, as late as 1800, the brother of the Austrian emperor reported that 90 percent of the peasants living within his own estate were pro-French.

Hapsburg authorities reacted to the menace of French revolutionary ideas by clamping down on their own people. Police surveillance expanded. Censors blocked the free spread of information. The church acquired additional power to make sure that all education followed traditional patterns. The government even made efforts to block economic growth because it feared change of any kind.

The conservative reaction worked for decades largely because of the brilliant leadership of the Austrian statesman Klemens von Metternich. Eventually resistance to change failed. Revolution in 1848 swept through Europe, and the Hapsburg Empire never fully recovered.

Austrian statesman Klemens von Metternich, in white coat, center, managed to keep Austria free of revolution until 1848. This anonymous colored engraving is from 1848.

SOUTHEASTERN EUROPE

The ripples of the French Revolution also reached southeastern Europe. This region had long been dominated by either the Hapsburg Empire or the Ottoman Empire (modern Turkey). Both these empires forcefully opposed change.

Three examples illustrate the plight of would-be reformers and rebels in southeastern Europe. Inspired by the French Revolution, during the 1790s, Serbs and Croats wanted to publish a newspaper to spread the news. They had to rely on printers in Vienna. The Austrian emperor allowed the newspapers to be printed only as long as they emphasized the evils of the French Revolution.

Likewise, the first Romanian newspaper was published in 1790. It featured news about the French Revolution. In response, a group of Romanians living in eastern Hungary, which was part of the Hapsburg Empire, sent a petition to Vienna asking for revolutionary, French-style changes. The Hapsburg government ignored the petition.

Greek nationalists also found inspiration in the French Revolution. At the time of the revolution (1789), Greece was part of the Ottoman Empire. One group of Greek nationalists plotted a revolt against the Turks. They drew up a constitution based on the French constitution of 1795. Austrian police arrested their leader and handed him over to Turkish authorities. The Turks, in turn, executed him.

REVOLUTIONS IN SOUTHERN EUROPE

During the Napoleonic Wars, an elected national assembly in Spain had drawn up a liberal constitution. It contained reforms inspired by the French Revolution. After allied forces drove the French from Spain, Spanish king Ferdinand VII returned to power in 1814. The Spanish National Assembly made the king promise to observe the

A NINETEENTH-CENTURY ENGRAVING DEPICTS THE ANNOUNCEMENT
OF "THE PROCLAMATION OF FERDINAND VII" IN MADRID IN 1814.
THE KING'S DECLARATION PROMISED A NEW CONSTITUTION.

new constitution. Instead, Ferdinand VII dissolved the assembly, discarded the constitution, and persecuted the liberal reformers.

Six years of poor government and corruption ensued. When an economic crisis came, conditions were ripe for revolt. The revolt began in 1820 in the military and quickly spread to upper-middle-class merchants. Liberal Spanish thinkers found intellectual support for the revolt when they considered the ideals of the French Revolution.

For a time, the radicals gained control. They modeled their efforts on the Jacobins of the French Revolution. A conservative reaction within Spain developed. Ironically, the Spanish conservatives required help from a French army to restore Ferdinand VII to power.

Inspired by the Spanish example, revolts broke out in other parts of southern Europe including Portugal and Italy. The Italian revolt

THE AFTERMATH OF THE FRENCH REVOLUTION

of 1820 initially centered on Naples. Just as had been the case in Spain, liberal reformers in Naples had created a new constitution during the Napoleonic Wars. When Ferdinand I returned to power in Naples, he promised to honor this constitution. Instead, just like his uncle, Ferdinand VII of Spain, he renounced the constitution. Just as had happened in Spain, first the army and then the merchant class revolted against the king's despotic rule.

Again the forces of reaction set in. This time Austria sent an army to Naples to restore Ferdinand I to power. Thereafter, the Austrian army marched north to subdue other Italian rebellions.

LATIN AMERICA

The French Revolution even influenced events in distant parts of the globe including Latin America. By the middle of the 1820s, all of the former Spanish colonies in South America had become independent republics. This was not a direct result of the French Revolution. However, the French Revolution had shown people worldwide that they could topple dynastic (hereditary) rule. South American rebels followed the French example. They issued declarations of rights and devised new constitutions, all of which used many of the thoughts and some of the language of the French Revolution.

The French Revolution is considered an important phase in human history. The Revolution taught many nations the lessons of freedom. It promoted the development of democracy and social reform as ideas of liberty and equality spread around the world. The Declaration of the Rights of Man and the Citizen had defined liberty as the right to do anything that did not harm others as long as others could also do the same. But it also meant freedom from arbitrary power, or the power of kings. And it meant freedom to think, write, and worship

The Slave Revolt in Haiti

DURING THE EARLY DAYS of the Revolution, French revolutionary leaders debated the issue of slavery. Did "liberté" and "égalité" apply to blacks? Even while the French legislature debated, the black slaves in one of France's colonies, Saint-Domingue (on the island of Hispaniola, modern Dominican Republic and Haiti) revolted against their white masters.

The Haitian revolt began on the island's sugar estates in August 1791. It grew into the largest and most successful slave revolt in history. On February 4, 1794, the National Convention in France abolished slavery in all French colonies and proclaimed that all men living in the colonies were French citizens with full rights.

This decision had a dramatic effect. Black rebel leaders, including Toussaint L'Ouverture (known as one of the fathers of the Haitian nation), rallied to the side of the French republic. However, other European powers, particularly Spain and Great Britain, relied on slavery to provide profits from the so-called Sugar Islands (the most important crop there was sugar, planted and harvested by black slaves). They became involved and the conflict continued.

When Napoléon Bonaparte became first consul, he restored slavery in the French colonies. Slavery officially persisted until 1848. However, because of the resistance of the blacks on Hispaniola, the French never reinstated slavery on that island. Instead, the former slaves on Saint-Domingue proclaimed the Republic of Haiti in 1804. The French Revolution had not caused the slave revolt in Haiti, but it had affected the outcome of that revolt.

in whatever way one wished. These values were not always upheld during the Revolution, especially during its worst days. And there were many of those. But they remained in the background, surfacing again and again. So it was that the French Revolution influenced so many other peoples and nations around the world.

The Legacy of the French Revolution

IN 1989 FRANCE CELEBRATED the two hundredth anniversary of the French Revolution. By this time, the Soviet empire's collapse was under way. Many French thinkers had considered the 1917 Russian Revolution, which established the Soviet Union, to be a desirable outgrowth of their own Revolution. The collapse of the Soviet empire made French thinkers reconsider not just the Russian Revolution but their own as well.

The legacy of the French Revolution—those momentous events that grew out of the revolution and its aftermath—can be seen in both a negative and a positive light. The historian Simon Schama concluded that the monarchy of Louis XVI ultimately fell because it was unable "to create representative institutions through which the state could execute its program of reform." In other words, the French government was unable to adapt to the desire of the common French citizens to have more say in their government. The various revolutionary governments were also unable to create such institutions. They debated how to do it and wrote fine-sounding speeches exploring new forms of government. But they too failed to devise a system of checks and balances among the branches of government. This failure meant that the only way to change the government was through violence.

The failure also meant that French citizens did not enjoy effective democratic representation. In other words, they had no voice in government. The Revolution had begun with an outline of the principles of liberal democracy. Yet by 1793–1794, it featured the extreme concentration of power. Moreover, those in power enjoyed almost unlimited rights to use that power.

The constitution of 1795 had created a two-chamber legislature. But only property owners could be elected to the legislature. While the Declaration of the Rights of Man and Citizen had pronounced that all citizens were entitled to participate in the political process, in reality, their participation was limited.

Likewise, the declaration had said that all citizens were free and equal, subject to law, free to own property, free to express opinions. In fact, during the Terror and again during Napoléon's reign, citizens did not enjoy these rights. The government exercised police power to forcibly deny French citizens the rights they had been promised.

French historians were more comfortable examining the aftermath of the Revolution in terms of positive changes. The Revolution's most uplifting legacy was its support for the concept of "human rights." The first article of the Declaration of the Rights of Man and Citizen stated that human beings are born free with equal rights. The second article said that the goal of political association was to preserve these rights. The French people could proudly link the modern struggle for human rights with their own revolutionary struggles.

An officer of the National Guard swears an Oath of Allegiance before the Altar of the Constitution of 1795. This French School oil painting is from the eighteenth century.

Social Changes

On the surface, one of the greatest social changes to result from the Revolution was the end of feudal rule. However, for the majority of the French people, this change did not hugely alter their lives. Instead of paying rent to lords of noble birth, peasants paid wealthy landlords. Instead of the king imposing taxes to pay off crippling war debts, Napoléon levied (collected) taxes to finance new wars.

The rural poor in particular gained very little from the Revolution. For example, before the Revolution, the Catholic Church owned large blocks of land. When the revolutionary government forced the sale of church property, it brought about a major transfer of wealth. But the people who acquired the property were not the poor or middle class. Rather, the wealthy, who already owned a fair amount of land, purchased the church property. The benefit of this transfer of wealth bypassed the poor.

Hereditary Privilege

Yet there were some very real gains for French citizens in the Revolution's aftermath. The Declaration of the Rights of Man and Citizen defined liberty as the right to do anything that did not harm others. It said that liberty also meant a person could expect freedom from arbitrary power. French revolutionaries perceived that they were fighting for human liberty. Their major foe was hereditary privilege as represented by kings. The attack against hereditary privilege is probably the most enduring legacy of the French Revolution. No longer could hereditary rulers simply cite hereditary right as the basis for their decisions. Absolute monarchs and dictators had to confirm their right to rule by appealing for popular support, or else they risked overthrow.

During the French Revolution and afterward, these appeals often featured rigged elections. Still, such elections opened the possibility that eventually rulers could not govern without the consent of the people.

The French Revolution asserted that the people—not kings, not hereditary elites, not the Catholic Church—were the rightful rulers. Within one hundred years, the peoples of Europe and the Americas accepted this notion.

POLITICAL CHANGES

Two new political ideologies emerged in the aftermath of the French Revolution: conservatism and liberalism. Conservatism aimed at

THE FRENCH REVOLUTION ASSERTED THAT THE PEOPLE—NOT KINGS OR HEREDITARY ELITES OR THE CATHOLIC CHURCH—WERE THE RIGHTFUL RULERS OF FRANCE. THIS FRENCH OIL PAINTING FROM 1790 SHOWS A GROUP OF DEMONSTRATING FRENCH CITIZENS.

preventing new upheavals, new revolutions. Liberalism promoted the idea that citizens are born with certain rights and have the right to try to influence their own future. According to historian William Doyle, liberalism specifically meant "representative government underpinned by a written constitution guaranteeing a basic range of human rights." These two ideologies, conservatism and liberalism, dominated European politics until late in the nineteenth century.

The Revolution also gave the world the political labels "left" and "right." Back when the assembly first convened, radicals sat together on one side, to the left of the leader's chair. Their opponents, the conservatives, sat on the right side of the leader. So it was that the political categories left and right came into being. Later, socialist thinkers rediscovered the labels left and right and brought them into wide use. Socialist politicians took over the label of "left wing." The left became associated with revolutionary change. The right became associated with opposition to such change. Today, the terms "left wing" and "right wing" are commonly used to describe political groups.

NATIONALISM

A new sense of national identity, the idea that citizens have a combination of rights from and duties to the nation in which they live, arose in the Revolution's aftermath. It replaced the ancient sense of national identity that emphasized the privileges (rights) of the rulers and only the duties of the citizens. But French revolutionary leaders called upon the entire nation, using the rallying cry "the fatherland in danger." Every able-bodied man had to fight. Everyone else had to work to support the war effort. France responded to this call. Nationalism, the modern sense of national identity, was born.

During the wars of the French Revolution and the Napoleonic Wars that followed, large patriotic French armies expanded French rule into neighboring regions. Nationalist spirit motivated the French expansion and influenced the development of nationalist spirit elsewhere too. Nationalist spirit caused people in Spain, Portugal, Italy, Austria, Germany, and Russia to mobilize for war against France. The French Revolution had unleashed the forces of nationalism across Europe. Once unleashed, these forces could not be contained. After the French Revolution, nationalism became the most important human political force in the world. The spirit of nationalism lies at the heart of the next 150 years of conflict and continues to exert enormous influence in the world of the twenty-first century.

MASS ARMIES

Before the French Revolution, the goal of warfare in Europe was usually for limited objectives. Small armies fought for control of a few fortress cities or for a small amount of territory. Then the war would end. When the French Revolution introduced nationalism to warfare, the nature of war changed.

For example, the levée en masse marked an enormous military change. Great Prussian military thinker Carl von Clausewitz, who had served as a soldier during the Napoleonic Wars, concluded, "In 1793 such a force as no one had any conception of made its appearance." To survive, the French Republic had mobilized all the nation's resources. To compete against France, other nations began to do the same. A female writer who lived through these times wrote: "The Revolution had brought the fatal art of recruiting to singular perfection." Her use of the term "fatal art" was well chosen. Future wars would not be more barbaric than those of the past. However, they would feature much larger armies recruited through mass conscription, and these armies would kill one another in unprecedented numbers.

REVOLUTION BY EXAMPLE

Because of the French example, the notion of revolution expanded to include the idea that people could also successfully rise up against foreign control of their homeland. All around the world, well into modern times, former colonies revolted to free themselves from colonial rule. Such revolts led to the creation of new governments and even new nations in Central and South America, Africa, and Asia. It helped inspire nationalists in Africa and Asia to revolt against their colonial masters. During the twentieth century, nationalists in such places as India, Algeria, and Vietnam expelled Europeans from their overseas colonies.

The leaders of the French Revolution could not have foreseen this outcome. However, if they had, they probably would have been content with the broad and enduring aftermath of the new social order they had launched in countries around the globe.

Timeline

1774	Louis XVI becomes the king of France.
June 17, 1789	The Third Estate declares the National Assembly.
July 14, 1789	Parisians storm the Bastille and dismantle the fortress, bringing about the first bloodshed of the French Revolution.
August 4, 1789	The National Constituent Assembly issues decrees that radically restructure French society and government.
August 1789	The assembly passes the Declaration of the Rights of Man and Citizens containing similar rights to those set forth in the U.S. Constitution.
October 7, 1789	A mob attacks Versailles, threatens the queen, and escorts Louis XVI to Paris, where he becomes a virtual prisoner in his palace.
July 1790	The assembly strips the Catholic Church of its property and power.
November 1790	The assembly requires a loyalty oath, which many Catholic clergy and citizens refuse to take.
June 20, 1791	The royal family tries to flee France but is captured and imprisoned in Paris. Moderates influence the assembly to acquit the king of any wrongdoing.

September 1791	The assembly adopts a new constitution that strips the king of most of his power.
April 20, 1792	The wars of the French Revolution begin with France's declaration of war against Austria.
June 1792	Prussia declares war on France.
September 2, 1792	The Parisian mob commits mass executions.
September 20–21, 1792	French soldiers stand firm at the battle of Valmy. The next day, France's constitutional convention votes to abolish the monarchy and declare France a republic.
January 21, 1793	Louis XVI is beheaded.
October 16, 1793	Marie Antoinette is beheaded.
September 1793– July 1794	During the Reign of Terror, an estimated twenty thousand people are executed, many on the merest suspicion of disloyalty to the Revolution.
July 28, 1794	The execution of Robespierre and his cronies marks the end of the Terror.
1795	France adopts a new constitution.
October 1795	Napoléon Bonaparte draws the favorable attention of the French government by commanding the artillery to open fire on a mob of royalist protesters.
September 1797	Members of the Directory (France's revolutionary government) mount a coup, reintroduce Terror laws, and return France to a virtual police state.

1798	France under the Directory expands military aggression against its neighbors, goading them to form a new alliance against France.
November 18–19, 1799	In the Coup of Brumaire, a conspiracy to overthrow the Directory, Napoléon Bonaparte seizes power.
December 25, 1799	Having dominated his coconspirators to become first consul, Napoléon presents a new national constitution that gives him enormous power.
March 27, 1802	Peace comes to France after French armies defeat the nations of the second coalition.
May 1803	War resumes between France and other European powers, beginning the Napoleonic Wars.
December 2, 1804	Bonaparte crowns himself Emperor Napoléon I, returning France to rule by a monarch with absolute power.
1815	Napoléon is defeated at the Battle of Waterloo in Belgium and is sent into permanent exile. Louis XVIII becomes king of France.

Glossary

aristocracy: those born into the noble class; in revolutionary France, they came to be seen as enemies of the people

artisan: skilled craftsman

assignat: paper currency of revolutionary France from 1790; it began steadily losing value

bourgeoisie: the middle class

counterrevolutionary: term applied to anyone suspected of being against the Revolution and desiring to return France to its former regime

coup: a sudden overthrow of the government; from the French words *coup d'état*, meaning a blow against the state

deputy: elected member of the French legislature

émigrés: people who emigrated from (left) revolutionary France; the term is applied to members of the aristocracy who plotted to overthrow the revolutionary government

Estates General: France's prerevolutionary representative body; it was made up of the Catholic clergy (the First Estate), the aristocracy (the Second Estate), and the rest of the country's population (the Third Estate)

feudalism: the system of land use in medieval Europe, under which serfs worked land that was owned by noblemen and paid part of their produce in rent

guilds: medieval trade organizations formed by skilled workers

levée en masse: a universal military draft declared in 1793 to support the French war effort

nationalism: the belief that the interests of one's nation are more important than other considerations

nobility: a hereditary privileged class; the aristocracy

patriot: a supporter of the aims of the Revolution; the French word *patrie* means "fatherland"

republicanism: a form of government in which a nation's leader is not a monarch and who, along with other government officials, is elected by the people

sansculottes: this French word literally means "without breeches"; it was originally used to make fun of the poor supporters of the revolution and later became a term to label all lower-class supporters of the revolution

the Terror: also called the Reign of Terror, this period lasted from September 1793 to July 1794, when the revolutionary government of France pursued a policy of identifying and killing suspected "enemies of the people." As the government broadened its definition of "enemy," people lived in terror of falling under suspicion.

Napoléon Bonaparte (1769–1821): Born Napoleone Buonaparte in Corsica (an island off the coast of Italy) to a family of modest means, the future conqueror of Europe was attending military school in France by the age of fifteen. He entered an artillery regiment the following year and in his spare time read and studied military history and science. He also shouldered much of the responsibility of supporting his widowed mother and eight younger siblings. Judged by history as one of only three "Great Captains," Napoléon's achievements in both military and government affairs have invited comparisons with Alexander the Great and Genghis Khan. He redrew the map of Europe with his conquests and formulated laws that still exist in modern France. Desperate for a legitimate son and heir to his empire, Napoléon divorced his beloved first wife, Empress Josephine, and married the young Marie-Louise of Austria in 1810. Napoléon II, born in 1811, returned with his mother to Austria on Napoléon's defeat in 1814 and was not permitted contact with his exiled father. Napoléon II died of tuberculosis at the age of twenty-two, leaving Napoléon I without legitimate descendants. Napoléon's mistress, Maria Walewska, bore him a son in 1810, from whom issued all direct descendants of Napoléon.

Georges-Jacques Danton (1759–1794): Educated as a lawyer, Georges Danton went into practice in Paris. At the beginning of the Revolution, he founded the radical Cordeliers Club and was a popular speaker at the Jacobins Club. Danton's influence over revolutionary politics grew until he became a leading figure in the founding of the French republic. He served in the revolutionary government and voted to execute Louis XVI. He became more moderate, however, during the Terror and tried to curb its excesses. This cost him his life.

Joseph Fouché (1759–1820): Though religious and unworldly in his youth, Fouché became one of the Revolution's most violent and ruthless leaders. As the Revolution began, he was in charge of a school run by a Catholic order. He began displaying his talent for identifying and allying himself with winners. He campaigned successfully for election to the National Convention, voted to condemn the king to death, and approved mass executions during the Terror. He switched his loyalties and served on the Directory, which he then plotted to overthrow. Fouché then became Napoléon's minister of police and ruthlessly destroyed Napoléon's enemies. When Napoléon fell, rose again, and fell yet again, Fouché nimbly switched loyalties between the emperor and the royal family. He served as minister of police under the Restoration as well, but was forced to retire when his condemnation of Louis XVI came back to haunt him. He died an immensely wealthy man.

Marquis de Lafayette (1757–1834): Marie-Joseph-Paul-Yves-Roch-Gilbert du Motier, known as the Marquis de Lafayette, was born in 1757 to a wealthy family. Orphaned at the age of thirteen, he joined the French army. He married at the age of sixteen, and at age nineteen crossed the Atlantic to support the American Revolution. Lafayette donated large sums of money, fought with the American army, and persuaded France to enter the war on the American side. During the French Revolution, he protected the king from the Paris mob. He was captured during the war with Austria and spent four years as a prisoner of war. Napoléon organized Lafayette's release in 1797.

Lafayette returned to France in 1800 and, with most of his wealth gone, retired to the countryside. He eventually reentered national politics and was instrumental in the 1830 overthrow of King Charles X. Lafayette died in 1834.

Louis XVI (1754–1793): A decent but weak-willed man, Louis Auguste de Bourbon became king of France in 1774 at the age of twenty. He had wed fourteen-year-old Marie Antoinette of Austria's Hapsburg dynasty when he was fifteen. The French and Austrian royal houses engineered the union in the attempt to join the two dynasties in friendship. Although the pair had little in common, Louis XVI was devoted to his wife. They eventually had four children, only one of whom survived to adulthood. Louis XVI was intelligent and well educated but ill prepared to rule a nation. His decision to assist the Americans in their fight for independence increased France's economic problems. During the Revolution, he failed to understand the need to either act decisively or compromise. Believing that the Revolution would fail, he took the advice of his wife and other members of his court to resist all change. He was beheaded in 1793.

Jean-Paul Marat (1743–1793): Marat spent many years in England as a respected physician and wrote several books on philosophical and political subjects. In 1777, he returned to France and was physician to prestigious and prosperous patients. In his spare time, he conducted scientific experiments with electricity and corresponded with American inventor and statesman Benjamin Franklin. Marat's failure to gain official recognition for his scientific work may have caused him to turn to politics and journalism, and he became editor of a revolutionary newspaper in 1789. Marat's views grew increasingly radical, and he advocated mass executions of counterrevolutionaries in his newspaper. On his election to the convention, he became one of its most powerful members. His assassination by Charlotte Corday at the height of his power led France to enshrine him as a martyr. So enduring was his fame that, more than a century later, the Soviet Russian navy named a battleship for him.

Marie Antoinette (1755–1793): The original name of the Austrian archduchess married to Louis XVI at the age of fourteen was Maria Antonia Josepha Joanna von Osterreich-Lothringen. The daughter of Holy Roman Emperor Francis I, she consoled herself for an indifferent marriage by spending large sums of money on frivolous amusements. She was fond of her husband but truly loved a Swedish military man. As an Austrian, she had few friends and many enemies in France, who circulated scandalous rumors about her. The resulting scandals and her real extravagance undercut the king's power. While the king wavered, Marie Antoinette acted decisively during the Revolution and arranged the failed escape attempt. Her secret communications with her family in Austria during that country's war with France fueled French hatred of the monarchy. Of the royal couple's four children, only one daughter lived to adulthood. That daughter, then a teenager, remained in prison after the king and queen went to the guillotine and was eventually sent to Austria as part of a prisoner exchange.

Maximilien Robespierre (1758–1794): Maximilien François Isidore de Robespierre was a lawyer who represented the Third Estate in the Estates General under the monarchy. However, he supported the formation of a republic, served in the subsequent National Assembly and Convention, and voted for the execution of Louis XVI. Robespierre became a leader of the Jacobins and ruthlessly implemented the Terror. When his fellow members of the convention themselves began to fear the Terror, they turned on Robespierre and had him executed. According to legend, he was placed face up in the guillotine (prisoners were typically placed face down).

Louis-Antoine-Léon de Saint-Just (1767–1794): As a teenager, Saint-Just ran away to Paris after a romantic disappointment in his hometown and quickly ran out of money. His mother had him seized, and he spent several months in a reformatory. He then trained as a lawyer but found the time to publish anonymously a book of erotic poetry. Saint-Just wanted to be elected to the National Assembly so he could serve the Revolution and champion the cause of the lower classes, but he had not yet reached the minimum age of twenty-five. When he attained that age, he was elected to the convention in 1792. He became a bold leader of the more radical elements, was elected president of the convention in 1794, and also led a successful military campaign against the Austrians. As Saint-Just gained power, he grew cold and ruthless. Once a principled campaigner for social justice, he became a bloodthirsty totalitarian monster. As a prime mover behind the Terror, he died on the guillotine along with Robespierre.

Charles Maurice de Talleyrand-Périgord (1754–1838): Talleyrand trained for the priesthood and rose through the ranks to become a bishop. He resigned from the clergy in 1791 to participate in revolutionary politics. He was appointed to serve on diplomatic missions to England and the United States and did not return to France until after the Terror, in 1795. Talleyrand became minister of foreign affairs under the Directory, but his talent for identifying winners led him to switch his loyalty to Napoléon. Years later, he foresaw Napoléon's fall, secretly negotiated with his enemies, and helped secure the throne of France for Louis XVIII. Talleyrand continued serving as a diplomat to two more French regimes, remaining active well into old age.

Source Notes

p. 4   Quoted in napoleonguide.com, "Execution of Louis XVI," n.d. <http://www.napoleonguide.com/guillotine_louis.htm> (accessed September 2006).

p. 5   Ibid.

p. 5   Ibid.

p. 6   Ibid.

p. 6   Quoted in Otto Scott, *Robespierre: The Fool as Revolutionary* (Windsor, NY: Reformer Library, 1995), 177.

p. 10   Emmanuel-Joseph Sieyès, "Essay on Privileges," in Marc Allan Goldstein, ed., *Social and Political Thought of the French Revolution 1788–1797: An Anthology of Original Texts* (New York: Peter Lang, 1997), 82, 90.

p. 13   Emmanuel-Joseph Sieyès, "What Is the Third Estate?" in Marc Allan Goldstein, ed., *Social and Political Thought of the French Revolution 1788–1797: An Anthology of Original Texts* (New York: Peter Lang, 1997), 106.

p. 15   Quoted in David Andress, *The Terror: The Merciless War for Freedom in Revolutionary France* (New York: Farrar, Straus and Giroux, 2005), 24.

p. 16   Quoted in Geoffrey Best, ed., *The Permanent Revolution: The French Revolution and Its Legacy* (Chicago: University of Chicago Press, 1988), 86.

p. 17 William Doyle, *The French Revolution: A Very Short Introduction* (Oxford: Oxford University Press, 2001), 44.

p. 18 Gouverneur Morris, *The Diary and Letters of Gouverneur Morris: Minister of the United States to France . . . etc.*, vol. 1, ed. Anne Cary Morris (New York: Charles Scribner's Sons, 1888), 137.

p. 20 Ibid., 168–169.

p. 20 Paul Thiébault, *The Memoirs of General Thiébault*, trans. Arthur John Butler (New York: Macmillan, 1896), 79.

p. 21 Quoted in Christopher Hibbert, *The Days of the French Revolution* (New York: William Morrow, 1980), 98.

p. 22 Thiébault, *The Memoirs of General Thiébault*, 82.

p. 25 Quoted in William Doyle, *The Oxford History of the French Revolution* (Oxford: Clarendon, 1989), 143.

p. 25 Ibid.

p. 40 Quoted in Simon Schama, *Citizens: A Chronicle of the French Revolution* (New York: Alfred A. Knopf, 1989), 640.

p. 41 Doyle, *The French Revolution*, 52.

p. 42 Etienne-Denis Pasquier, *The Memoirs of Chancellor Pasquier, 1767–1815*, trans. Douglas Garman (Cranbury, NJ: Fairleigh Dickinson University Press, 1968), 39.

p. 46 Quoted in Wilfred B. Kerr, *The Reign of Terror 1793–1794* (Toronto: University of Toronto Press, 1927), 186.

p. 49   *Internet Modern History Sourcebook*, "The *Lévee en Masse*, August 23, 1793." n.d. <http://www.fordham.edu/halsall/mod/1793levee.html> (accessed August 2006).

p. 52   Quoted in David Chandler, *The Campaigns of Napoleon* (New York: Macmillan, 1966), 68.

p. 53   Quoted in Andress, *The Terror*, 179.

p. 54   A.C. Thibaudeau, *Mémoires*, vol. 1 (Paris: Baudouin Frères, 1824), 44.

p. 55   Andress, *The Terror*, 212.

p. 59   *Internet Modern History Sourcebook*, "The *Lévee en Masse*, August 23, 1793." n.d. <http://www.fordham.edu/halsall/mod/1793levee.html> (accessed August 2006).

p. 59   Joseph Fouché, "Directive Addressed to the Constitutional Authorities of the Department of the Rhone and Loire by the Temporary Commission," in Marc Allan Goldstein, ed., *Social and Political Thought of the French Revolution 1788–1797: An Anthology of Original Texts* (New York: Peter Lang, 1997), 504–505.

p. 62   Quoted in Hibbert, *The Days of the French Revolution*, 227.

p. 62   Quoted in Norman Hampson, *Danton* (New York: Holmes & Meier, 1978), 142.

p. 62   Quoted in Hibbert, *The Days of the French Revolution*, 235.

pp. 63–64 Ibid., 236.

p. 65   Quoted in Andress, *The Terror*, 289.

p. 65   Thibaudeau, *Mémoires*, 60.

p. 65   Quoted in Hampson, *Danton*, 174.

p. 65   Ibid.

p. 65   Quoted in Hibbert, *The Days of the French Revolution*, 248.

p. 66   *Internet Modern History Sourcebook*, "Maximilien Robespierre: On the Principles of Political Morality, February 1794." n.d. <http://www.fordham.edu/halsall/mod/1794robespierre.html> (accessed August 2006).

p. 68   Thibaudeau, *Mémoires*, 50.

p. 68   Joe H. Kirchberger, *The French Revolution and Napoleon: An Eyewitness History* (New York: Facts On File, 1989), 119.

pp. 68–69 Anne-Louise-Germaine de Staël, *Considerations on the Principal Events of the French Revolution*, vol. 1, translated from the original manuscript (New York: James Eastburn, 1818), 357–358.

p. 71   Quoted in Kirchberger, *The French Revolution and Napoleon* , 121.

pp. 71–72 Ibid., 156.

p. 74   Quoted in Hibbert, *The Days of the French Revolution*, 285.

p. 76   Quoted in Chandler, *The Campaigns of Napoleon*, 56.

p. 79   Quoted in Hibbert, *The Days of the French Revolution*, 247–248.

p. 77   Quoted in Kirchberger, *The French Revolution and Napoleon*, 157.

p. 77   Ibid, 158.

p. 82   Charles Talleyrand-Périgord, *The Memoirs of Prince Talleyrand*, vol. 1 (New York: G. P. Putnam's Sons, 1891), 194.

p. 82   Quoted in Kirchberger, *The French Revolution and Napoleon*, 159.

p. 83   Pasquier, *Memoirs of Chancellor Pasquier*, 48.

p. 84   Quoted in James R. Arnold, *Marengo and Hohenlinden: Napoleon's Rise to Power* (Lexington, VA: Napoleon Books, 1999), 7.

p. 85   Ibid.

p. 86   Quoted in Will and Ariel Durant, *The Age of Napoleon* (New York: Simon & Schuster, 1975), 199.

p. 86   Napoléon Bonaparte, "To the French," December 15, 1799, in *Correspondance de Napoléon Ier*, vol. 6 (Paris: H. Plon, J. Dumaine, 1860), 25.

pp. 89–90 François Chateaubriand, *The Memoirs of Chateaubriand*, trans. Robert Baldick (New York: Alfred A Knopf, 1961), 262–263.

p. 91   Ibid., 267.

p. 91   Quoted in J. Christopher Herold, *The Mind of Napoleon* (New York: Columbia University Press, 1955), 43, 73.

p. 93   Quoted in Chandler, *The Campaigns of Napoleon*, 53.

pp. 95–96   Charles James Fox, *Memorials and Correspondence of Charles James Fox*, vol. 2 (New York: AMS, 1970), 361.

p. 96   Quoted in Doyle, *The Oxford History of the French Revolution*, 160–161.

p. 97   Quoted in Margery Weiner, *The French Exiles 1789–1815* (London: John Murray, 1960), 71.

p. 102   Quoted in Robert R. Palmer, *The World of the French Revolution* (New York: Harper & Row, 1967), 236.

p. 103   Quoted in Charles Breunig, *The Age of Revolution and Reaction, 1789–1850* (New York: W. W. Norton, 1977), 44.

p. 108   Quoted in Best, *The Permanent Revolution*, 14.

p. 113   Quoted in Palmer, *The World of the French Revolution*, 135.

p. 113   Ibid., 138.

p. 114   Ibid., 147.

p. 123   Simon Schama, *Citizens: A Chronicle of the French Revolution* (New York: Alfred A. Knopf. 1989), 857.

p. 128   Doyle, *The French Revolution*, 82–83.

p. 129   Quoted in Doyle, *The Oxford History of the French Revolution*, 416.

p. 129   Staël, *Considerations on the Principal Events of the French Revolution*, 76.

Bibliography

Andress, David. *The Terror: The Merciless War for Freedom in Revolutionary France*. New York: Farrar, Straus and Giroux, 2005.

Arnold, James R. *Marengo and Hohenlinden: Napoleon's Rise to Power*. Lexington, VA: Napoleon Books, 1999.

Best, Geoffrey, ed. *The Permanent Revolution: The French Revolution and Its Legacy*. Chicago: University of Chicago Press, 1988.

Breunig, Charles. *The Age of Revolution and Reaction, 1789–1850*. New York: W.W. Norton, 1977.

Cappon, Lester J., ed. *The Adams-Jefferson Letters*. 2 vols. Chapel Hill: University of North Carolina Press, 1959.

Chandler, David. *The Campaigns of Napoleon*. New York: Macmillan, 1966.

Chateaubriand, François. *The Memoirs of Chateaubriand*. Translated by Robert Baldick. New York: Alfred A. Knopf, 1961.

Doyle, William. *The French Revolution: A Very Short Introduction*. Oxford: Oxford University Press, 2001.

———. *The Oxford History of the French Revolution*. Oxford: Clarendon, 1989.

Fox, Charles James. *Memorials and Correspondence of Charles James Fox*. 4 vols. New York: AMS, 1970.

Gershoy, Leo. *The Era of the French Revolution: 1789–1799*. Princeton: D. Van Nostrand, 1957.

Goldstein, Marc Allan, ed. *Social and Political Thought of the French Revolution 1788–1797: An Anthology of Original Texts*. New York: Peter Lang, 1997.

Hampson, Norman. *Danton*. New York: Holmes & Meier, 1978.

Hibbert, Christopher. *The Days of the French Revolution*. New York: William Morrow, 1980.

Kerr, Wilfred B. *The Reign of Terror 1793–4*. Toronto: University of Toronto Press, 1927.

Kirchberger, Joe H. *The French Revolution and Napoleon: An Eyewitness History*. New York: Facts On File, 1989.

Macdonald, Etienne. *Recollections of Marshal Macdonald*, I. Translated by Stephen Louis Simeon. New York: Charles Scribner's Sons, 1893.

Morris, Gouverneur. *The Diary and Letters of Gouverneur Morris: Minister of the United States to France . . . etc.* Vol. 1. Edited by Anne Cary Morris. New York: Charles Scribner's Sons, 1888.

Palmer, Robert R. *The World of the French Revolution*. New York: Harper & Row, 1967.

Pasquier, Etienne-Denis. *Memoirs of Chancellor Pasquier, 1767-1815*. Translated by Douglas Garman. Cranbury, NJ: Fairleigh Dickinson University Press, 1968.

Roger, Alexander B. *The War of the Second Coalition*. Oxford: Clarendon, 1964.

Schama, Simon. *Citizens: A Chronicle of the French Revolution*. New York: Alfred A. Knopf, 1989.

Scott, Otto. *Robespierre: The Fool as Revolutionary*. Windsor, NY: Reformer Library, 1995.

Staël, Anne-Louise-Germaine de. *Considerations on the Principal Events of the French Revolution.* 2 vols., translated from the original manuscript. New York: James Eastburn, 1818.

Talleyrand-Périgord, Charles. *The Memoirs of Prince Talleyrand.* 2 vols. New York: G. P. Putnam's Sons, 1891.

Thibaudeau, A. C. *Mémoires.* 2 vols. Paris: Baudouin Frères, 1824.

Thiébault, Paul. *The Memoirs of General Thiébault.* Translated by Arthur John Butler. New York: Macmillan, 1896.

La Tour du Pin, Henrietta Lucy de. *Memoirs.* London: Harvill, 1999.

Weiner, Margery. *The French Exiles 1789–1815.* London: John Murray, 1960.

For Further Reading and Websites

BOOKS

Bohannon, Lisa Frederiksen. *The American Revolution*. Minneapolis: Twenty-First Century Books, 2004. This title explores the background to and the history of the war between Great Britain and her thirteen American colonies. The colonies gained their independence, becoming the new nation known as the United States.

Chandler, David. *The Campaigns of Napoleon*. New York: Macmillan, 1966. The late Dr. Chandler was the foremost English-language authority on the Napoleonic Wars.

Dickens, Charles. *A Tale of Two Cities*. New York: Signet Classics, 2007. This classic 1859 novel of the French Revolution has been published in countless editions and is widely available.

Fraser, Antonia. *Marie Antoinette: The Journey*. New York: Doubleday, 2001. This biographer shows great sympathy for her subject, a fourteen-year-old girl married off to the future king of France, forced to endure brutal treatment, who nevertheless goes to her execution with courage and dignity.

Hanson, Paul R. *Historical Dictionary of the French Revolution*. Lanham, MD: Scarecrow, 2004. This is a handy reference to the French Revolution. Entries are listed alphabetically. An extensive bibliography provides readers with other sources for further research.

Landau, Elaine. *Napoleon Bonaparte*. Minneapolis: Twenty-First Century Books, 2006. This biography describes the life of one of the world's most brilliant military leaders, who became dictator of France.

WEBSITES

The French Revolution
<http://www.schoolhistory.co.uk/year8links/frenchrevolution.shtml>
This British resource guide reflects the British point of view of the French Revolution.

The French Revolution
<http://www.infoplease.com/ce6/history/A0819666.html>
This source of general information from Pearson Education's infoplease site is easy to navigate. It contains many easy-to-read articles about different aspects of the French Revolution.

The French Revolution
<http://www.fordham.edu/halsall/mod/modsbook13.html>
This section of Fordham University's site provides a collection of original documents and Web links pertaining to the revolutionary and Napoleonic periods.

The French Revolution & Napoleon
<http://members.aol.com/TeacherNet/FrRev.html>
This easy-to-navigate site is devoted to the French Revolution and Napoléon and provides links to other related sites as well.

Napoleonic Guide
<http://www.napoleonguide.com>
This basic guide to Napoleonic information includes movies, DVDs, and books.

The Napoleon Series
<www.napoleon-series.org>
The International Napoleonic Society presents information on the life and times of Napoléon Bonaparte.

Index

governments: adaptability to desires of people of, 123–124; under constitution of 1795, 71–74, 77, 93, 124; empire, 93; factions in, 72–73, 84; list of different, 93; under Louis XVI, 12; restructuring by National Constituent Assembly of, 23

Great Britain: after defeat of Austria, 76; and American Revolution, 6–7; and coalitions against France, 78, 87, 90–91; declared war against France, 43; and defeat of Napoléon, 90–91; and Haiti, 122; and invasion of Brittany by émigrés, 71; and Ireland, 109–111; navy of, 48, 52; political impact of French Revolution on, 96–99

Great Terror, 65–68

Greece, 119

guerrilla fighters, 43, 51

Guillotin, Joseph-Ignace, 60

guillotine, 60

habeas corpus in Great Britain, 98–99

Haiti, 122

Hapsburg Empire, 100–102, 106, 116–119. *See also* Austria

Hébertists, 61–62, 73

Helvetic Republic, 106

hereditary privilege, 126–127

Holland, 101–102. *See also* Dutch Republic

Holy Roman Empire, 101

human rights, 124

Hungary, 117, 119

Ireland, 109–111

Italian states: effect of Revolutionary and Napoleonic Wars on, 101, 106–108, 120–121; as member of coalition against France, 43, 89

Jacobins: coup against Directory by, 79; described, 26, 73; as dominant faction during Terror, 53–54; and king, 27; and Robespierre, 67; and Russian Revolution, 116; and sansculottes, 44; and Spanish Revolution, 120; and Thermidoreans, 70

Jemappes, Battle of, 100

Joseph Leopold II (emperor of Austria), 30–32

Kosciuszko, Thaddeus, 112

Lafayette, Marquis de, 21, 92

land: belonging to Catholic Church, 126; ownership limits, 54, 71–72; ownership prior to Revolution, 9; and voting rights, 37, 124

Latin America, 121–122

Launay, Bernard de, 15

Law of 22 Prairial, 65, 68

Law of Suspects, 54–55

Lefebvre, François, 83–84

left wing, 128

legal code, 88, 94

Legislative Assembly: decree against émigrés and clergy by, 29; described, 93; members of, 28; monarchy suspended by, 39; and Revolutionary Wars, 30–34, 36–37, 39

levée en masse (mass conscription), 48, 49–51, 129

liberalism, 128

Lisle, Claude-Joseph Rouget de, 35

Louis, Antoine, 60

Louis-Philippe (king of France), 92–94

Louis XVIII (king of France), 93; attempted assassination of Napoléon by, 87; and background to Revolutionary Wars, 30–32; return as king of, 91

Louis XVI (king of France): and bread demands, 21; conditions during reign of, 8–9; as constitutional monarch,

Photo Acknowledgments

The images in this book are used with the permission of: Réunion des Musées Nationaux / Art Resource, N.Y., 5; © Roger Viollet / The Image Works, 11, 33, 50, 115, 127; Getty Images, 14; © Visual Arts Library (London) / Alamy, 16, 22; Bildarchiv Preussischer Kulturbesitz / Art Resource, N.Y., 24; © Classic Image / Alamy, 27; © Mary Evans Picture Library / Alamy, 29; © INTERPHOTO Pressebildagentur / Alamy, 31; Erich Lessing / The Image Works, 35; Steve Zmina, 38; © The Print Collector / Alamy, 41, 76; Henri de La Rochejaquelein (1772-94) at the Battle of Cholet, 17th October 1793 (oil on canvas), Boutigny, Paul Emile (1854-1929) / Musée d'Histoire, Cholet, France, Giraudon / The Bridgeman Art Library, 44; © The Gallery Collections / Corbis, 47; © Mary Evans Picture Library / The Image Works, 55, 67, 104; The Art Archive / Musées Carnavale: Paris / Marc Charmet, 57, 60; Hulton Archive / Getty Images, 64, 112; Giraudon / Art Resource, N.Y.,69, 92; Erich Lessing / Art Resource, N.Y., 83, 85, 107; The Art Archive / Musées du Châteaux de Versailles / Gianni Dagli Orti, 88, 118; © Lebrecht Music & Arts / The Image Works, 97; The Republican Attack, published by Hannah Humphrey in 1795 (hand-coloured etching), Gillray, James (1757-1815) / © Courtesy of the Warden and Scholars of New College, Oxford, / The Bridgeman Art Library, 99; © Gianni Dagli Orti / Corbis, 100; The United Irish Patriots of 1798, pub. 1898 (litho), Irish School, (19th century) / Private Collection, / The Bridgeman Art Library, 110; Popperfoto / Getty Images, 116; © Archivo Iconografico, S.A. / Corbis, 120; An Officer of the National Guard Swearing an Oath of Allegiance before the Altar of the Constitution and the Declaration of the Rights of Man (oil on canvas), French School, (18th century) / Private Collection, Lauros / Giraudon / The Bridgeman Art Library, 125.

Front Cover © The Bridgeman Art Library / Getty Images

About the Author

James R. Arnold has written more than twenty-five political history and military history books on topics ranging from the Napoleonic Wars to the origins of the American involvement in Vietnam. Arnold is currently serving as managing editor for the *Journal of Military History*, providing historical content and analysis for a database on the role of wars in U.S. history, and is writing a history of counterinsurgency.